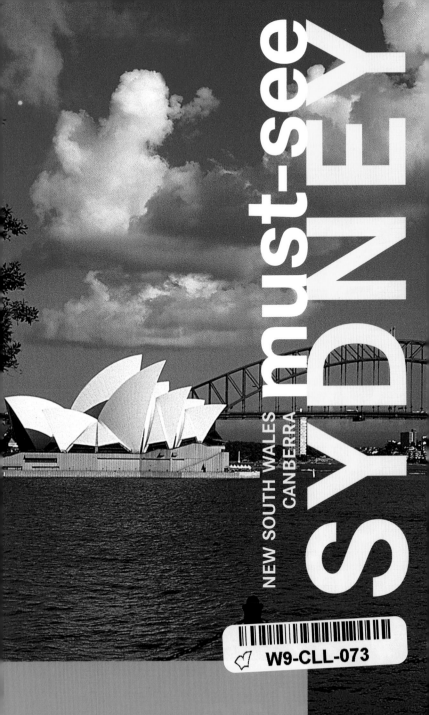

must-see SYDNEY

NEW SOUTH WALES
CANBERRA

W9-CLL-073

KERRY FISHER

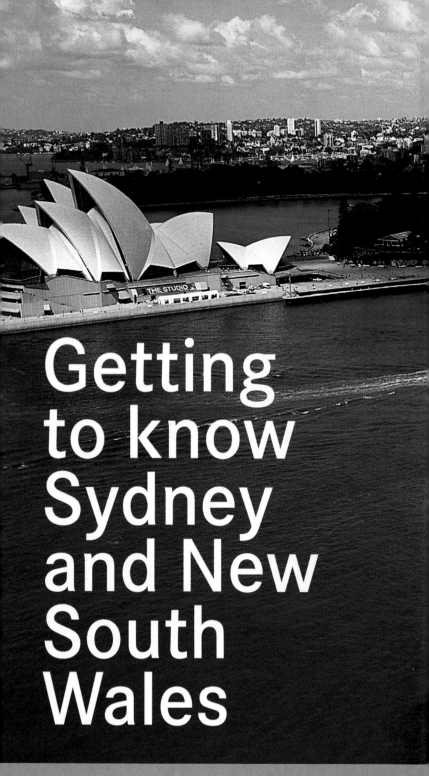

Getting to know Sydney and New South Wales

must-see
SYDNEY
NEW SOUTH WALES | CANBERRA

CONTENTS

Published by Thomas Cook Publishing
The Thomas Cook Group Ltd
PO Box 227, Thorpe Wood
Peterborough PE3 6PU
United Kingdom

Telephone: 01733 503571
E–mail: books@thomascook.com

Text: © The Thomas Cook Group Ltd 2000
Maps: © The Thomas Cook Group Ltd 2000

ISBN 1 841570 47 8

Distributed in the United States of America by the Globe Pequot Press,
PO Box 480, Guilford, Connecticut 06437, USA.

Distributed in Canada by Whitecap Books, 351 Lynn Avenue,
North Vancouver, British Columbia, Canada V7J 2C4.

Distributed in Australia and New Zealand by Peribo Pty Limited,
58 Beaumont Road, Mt Kuring-Gai, NSW, 2080, Australia.

Publisher: Stephen York
Commissioning Editor: Deborah Parker
Map Editor: Bernard Horton

Series Editor: Christopher Catling

Written and researched by: Kerry Fisher

Cover photograph: Ethel Davies

GETTING TO KNOW SYDNEY AND NEW SOUTH WALES

Discovering Sydney and New South Wales

As long ago as the 1850s, Australian unions were campaigning for an eight-hour working day, with the slogan '8 hours' labour, 8 hours' recreation, 8 hours' rest'. That fiercely guarded balance between work and play still holds true today, which, for the tourist, means that Sydney's possibilities for fun and R&R are endless.

Sydney is an important business centre, but there's none of that overwhelming, overcrowded, stressed-out feel usually associated with major cities. You don't have to brace yourself to step out into the fray. The roads and pavements are wide, there are plenty of parks and the glorious harbour gives the city a feeling of space. For every tight-lipped, scurrying executive, there's another city dweller lingering over lunch alfresco, enjoying a mid-morning cappuccino at Hyde Park café or rollerblading in Centennial Park. Some areas of Sydney are purely recreational – Darling Harbour is the ultimate waterfront playground with top quality museums, restaurants and shops. Even Martin Place at the heart of the business district echoes with the sound of lunchtime bands.

Jan Morris wrote in her acerbic, yet affectionate account of Sydney: 'Young people coming from Britain, in particular, immediately feel a sense of euphoric hope and liberty.' Whether that's confined only to young Brits is a matter of opinion, but there's something very liberating about swapping busy shopping malls for the golden beaches of Manly, just a scenic ferry ride away. Life feels unconstrained, as though anything's possible. Where else could tourists wander in and out of the House of Parliament as though it were a public library? Or climb a national monument such as the Harbour Bridge? As one American tourist put it, the fear of litigation would be too great.

National anthem

Australians all let us rejoice,
For we are young and free;
We've golden soil and wealth for toil;
Our home is girt by sea;
Our land abounds in nature's gifts
Of beauty rich and rare;
In history's page, let every stage
Advance Australia Fair.

Undoubtedly, Sydney's sunny climate for over 90 per cent of the year contributes to this sense of freedom. People live outdoors. Workers don't head home for an evening spent cooped up over the laptop. They're at the open-air cinema in Centennial Park, enjoying a post-work dip at Bondi or catching a classical concert on the Domain.

" *As I stood in the Botanic Gardens looking at the harbour, I realised that was the view people had on migrant ships and even if all they had was one little cardboard suitcase, they were arriving in what looked like Utopia.* "

Marele Day, Australian crime writer, *Places in the Heart* (1997, Hodder Headline)

Holidaymakers whose preconceptions of Sydney are hazy images of the Opera House, Harbour Bridge, barbecues and cork hats are in for a reality check. Sydney's architecture is more than just the harbourside greats. There's the convict-built Rocks, Paddington's Victorian terraces, the Francis Greenway masterpieces on Macquarie St. The food is excellent and utterly cosmopolitan, with yum cha in Chinatown, tapas in Liverpool St and anything from noodles to bratwurst and satay in Darlinghurst. And whilst it's true that Aussies favour casual clothes, a browse round Paddington's boutiques and the city-centre designer dens puts Sydney on a par with any other major city.

Beyond Sydney, the surprises keep coming. First, the countryside is so vast that you can drive for kilometres without seeing another car. Secondly, the landscape and towns offer so much contrast. Misty rainforest trails and rugged coastal paths. Skiing in the mountains, surfing at deserted beaches. Galleries and antique shops in quaint colonial villages, huge department stores in modern shopping malls. Ultra-slick vineyards, spit and sawdust, two barrels and a bunch of grapes wineries. Purpose-built hi-tech theme parks, unspoilt national parks with aboriginal engravings. Bushwalks in the company of kangaroos, parrots and wallabies, late-night dancing to local rock bands.

Whatever your holiday hopes, whatever your style, taste or budget, Sydney and NSW have it all and more, uncrowded, accessible and unique.

A day in the life of Sydney

Rudyard Kipling (1865–1936) wrote that 'Sydney . . . was populated by leisured multitudes all in shirt sleeves and all picnicking all the day'. Whilst today's modern city has its fair share of harassed-looking executives, you never shake off the feeling that work is peripheral and the city's population conserves most of its energy for an attractive outdoor lifestyle and a huge amount of post-work fun. Here's what they do:

0500 Still primped and pouting, although the mascara may be a little smudged, Sydney's nightclub body beautifuls spill out onto Oxford St to greet the morning after a hard night's techno dancing.

0730 The city's cafés start to fill up as workers pop in for a flat white or short black caffeine shot, a wholesome muffin, ginger and carrot juice and a flick through the *Sydney Morning Herald.*

0805 The first keen tourists are being breathalysed before they embark on their climb to the top of Sydney, up the Harbour Bridge.

0830 The Central Business District (CBD) is already buzzing with smart-suited financiers, whilst ferries are crowding into Circular Quay with commuters from Balmain, Mosman and Manly.

1230 City workers congregate in Martin Place to enjoy the free lunchtime concerts, others buy a focaccia sandwich and picnic under the shady trees in the Domain, Hyde Park or the Royal Botanic Gardens.

1430 At Sydney Oyster Cove, tourists are still lingering over a lunch of Sydney rock oysters and savouring the views over the

harbour. East of the city, Bondi is buzzing with daredevil surfers, skateboarders, itsy bitsy bikinis and tanned torsos.

1730 Office workers pop into the bottle shop on their way home for a pack of VB beers or a chilled chardonnay. Young professionals rush to David Jones Food Hall before it closes at 1800 to pick up succulent seafood and antipasti from the mouth-watering deli.

1830 The city's jogging fraternity put themselves through their paces along the scenic Bondi to Coogee coastal path, the Manly to Spit walkway and the harbourside walk from the Opera House to Mrs Macquarie's Chair.

1900 Those in search of dinner with views take a sunset cruise on the harbour, whilst cocktail fans head to the Horizon Bar at the top of the ANA Hotel in Cumberland St for unrivalled, budget-busting views over city's landmarks.

2000 Music buffs enjoy outdoor jazz and symphonies on the Domain during the Sydney Festival in January.

2030 The restaurant-lined streets of Kings Cross and Darlinghurst are bustling with customers sampling everything from spicy Thai curries to Austrian goulash and Mod Oz seared and sundried creations. Ultra trendies wine and dine at Sydney's new Cockle Bay Wharf.

2130 The gay bars around Taylor Square and Oxford St are revving up for the night, Kings Cross flashes with raunchy neon signs, whilst beer boozers head to the Mercantile, the Lord Nelson and the Hero of Waterloo at the Rocks.

2330 The first trickle of the near naked painted dolls, concave lycra-clad stomachs and tightly trousered butts wend their way to the bop-till-dawn nightclubs around Oxford St and the CBD.

0130 The drunk, the starving and the insomniacs head to the Sydney institution of Harry's brightly coloured Café de Wheels van to fill up on one of his infamous pies and pasties served up with peas.

" *Australia is a weird, big country. It feels so empty and untrodden . . . even Sydney, which is huge, begins to feel unreal, as if life here really had never entered in: as if it were just sprinkled over and the land lay untouched.* "

D H Lawrence's impression of Australia in the 1920s

9

Yesterday and tomorrow

Sydney has all the hallmarks of a cosmopolitan, modern city. Yet just over 200 years ago, Australia was an untamed wilderness, populated by aborigines living there virtually undisturbed for around 60,000 years.

Early days

From the 15th century onwards, several European countries flirted with discovery of a southern land but it was the English who claimed possession in 1770, when **Captain Cook** landed on the east coast in the *Endeavour*.

The American War of Independence deprived Britain of a place to transport her criminals, so by 1788 convicts were being shipped off to Sydney where they struggled to survive.

The city's fortunes improved under **Lachlan Macquarie**, governor of the colony from 1810, whose progressive policies led to a programme of convict-built public buildings and prisoner emancipation.

The colony blossoms

From the 1830s, free settlers were encouraged to the colony with assisted passages. In 1840, convict transportation to NSW ended. Meanwhile the colony was developing rapidly: in 1813 a route was found across the **Blue Mountains** to the fertile western plains, railways were built from the 1850s and gold was discovered at **Bathurst** in 1851.

Into the 20th century

In 1901, NSW united with Australia's other colonies to form a federation, the Commonwealth of Australia, eventually establishing a federal capital in **Canberra**.

The first half of the century offered mixed fortunes – many of NSW's young men were amongst the 60,000 Australians killed in World War I. Over 8500 were killed at Gallipoli alone. A national holiday (25 April) commemorates the **Anzac** (Australian and New Zealand Army Corps) landing there in 1915, widely regarded as Australia's 'coming of age'.

The 1920s started well – 300,000 Brits emigrated to Sydney, construction of the Harbour Bridge began – before falling wool and wheat prices plunged the country into depression. The 1940s saw Australia embroiled in World War II, followed by a massive post-war British and European immigration boom. By the 1970s attitudes were changing – the Labour party came to power after an absence of over 20 years, Australian troops were withdrawn from Vietnam, aboriginal land rights, free education and urban conservation were high on the agenda. The 1980s was a period of economic upswing with extensive **bicentennial celebrations** in 1988, followed by recession in the early 1990s.

Into the millennium

In September 2000, Sydney will host the greenest **Olympic Games** ever. The NSW government has splashed out $2.3 billion on Olympic venues, related services and construction, with private investors spending millions more.

Pre-millennium developments include a 'Living City' programme designed to make Sydney a more enjoyable place to live. Central to this is the construction of the $35 million **Cook and Phillip Park** (*College St*) in the centre of Sydney. Australia holds a referendum in November 1999 on whether to abandon the Queen in favour of a republic in 2001. Opinion polls indicate that it will choose to march into the 21st century independent of Britain at last.

People and places

Australians are straightforward people, who are generally unimpressed by wealth, success or status. Indeed, very successful people are known as 'Tall Poppies', ripe for being chopped down. However, here are a few figures who've dared to poke their noses above the parapet.

The media men

Australia was the birthplace of **Rupert Murdoch**, one of the most prolific media moguls in the world. His extensive empire includes the *New York Post*, the English newspapers the *Sun* and *The Times*, the satellite Fox Network and Star TV. He also owns the Los Angeles Dodgers baseball team and tried (and failed) to buy the English football team, Manchester United. He regularly clashes horns with his arch rival, Kerry Packer, the richest man in Australia, who owns an enormous TV and magazine empire.

The creative creatures

Sydney has a vibrant arts scene with many artists, designers, actors and writers gaining inspiration on her harbour shores. The star of the current fashion scene is **Collette Dinnigan**, famed for her wispy feminine creations, popular with celebrities such as Jerry Hall and Paula Yates. Her reputation was assured when Australian supermodel Sarah O'Hare requested a wedding dress for her marriage to Murdoch's son, Lachlan.

If Dinnigan is subtle, Sydney's best-known artist, **Ken Done**, is striking. He has achieved immense commercial success by translating bright, simple images into murals – see the **Powerhouse Garden Restaurant** (*page 49*) – T-shirts and table mats as well as traditional paintings.

NSW has always had strong literary connections, with many writers (**D H Lawrence, Jack London, Rudyard**

Kipling) visiting from overseas, and plenty of homegrown talent. Back in the 1890s, the *Bulletin* was famous for encouraging Australian bushmen to contribute literary offerings about life in the outback. Two of the state's poets, **Banjo Paterson** (1864–1941), best known for writing the words to *Waltzing Matilda*, and **Henry Lawson** (1867–1922), (buried in Bronte's Waverley Cemetery), competed with each other through its pages.

NSW-born **Miles Franklin** (1879–1954), author of *My Brilliant Career* (1901) and ardent feminist, lends her name to the most prestigious literary award in Australia. **Germaine Greer**, who studied at Sydney University, found worldwide fame with her book *The Female Eunuch* (1970). In 1973, **Patrick White** (1912–90) from the Southern Highlands won the Nobel Prize for Literature with *The Eye of the Storm*.

The stars of the silver screen are also well represented in Sydney: **Nicole Kidman** grew up in the city's suburbs, **Mel Gibson** spent his teenage years there, **Paul Hogan** of *Crocodile Dundee* fame worked as a painter on the Harbour Bridge and the Down Under's latest hot property, actress **Cate Blanchett** (star of *Elizabeth*), went to drama school there.

The politicians

Gough Whitlam was the first Labour Prime Minister to be elected since 1949 when he came to power in 1972. His government introduced a programme of social reform such as free university education and a national health system. However, amidst rising inflation and accusations of loan mismanagement, Whitlam's government was sacked in 1975 by the Queen's representative in Australia, the Governor-General, a crisis which is often pinpointed as the catalyst for a serious republican movement. Currently, Australia's Prime Minister is **John Howard** (Liberal), popular with the country's middle classes for his conservative policies and squeaky-clean image, although many feel that he lacks the charisma of his predecessor, **Paul Keating** (Labour). The Premier of NSW, **Bob Carr** (Labour) was returned to office for a further term in 1999 with Labour's biggest landslide win since 1978.

Getting around

Sydney's combination of inexpensive buses, trains and ferries ensures that a ride near to where you want to go is never far away. Unless you are a very confident driver, public transport is infinitely preferable within the city, which is a maze of one-way streets and meter parking.

Air

The main domestic airlines are **Ansett** and **Qantas**, which fly to several regional airports all over NSW. Internal flights are not cheap but production of your international ticket will entitle you to a substantial discount.

Buses

The **Sydney Buses** service is generally good. Buses with numbers prefaced by X or E (for express) or L (for limited) are the quickest as they make fewer stops. Buy tickets from the driver or validate your pass in the machine. The main bus terminals are at Alfred St by Circular Quay (for buses south, west and east), York St at Wynyard and by the Queen Victoria Building (for buses north) and Elizabeth St (for those going east).

Car

If you want to explore the more remote national parks and inland towns, then a car is a must. Major companies such as Avis, Hertz, Budget and Thrifty have outlets all over NSW. If you're starting from Sydney, head to William St,

home to all the big companies plus a few smaller outfits. Most contracts include a mileage allowance of 100km per day – distances are huge in Australia, so consider paying a bit more for unlimited mileage. You have to be over 21 and all policies include an excess (much greater for drivers under 25), which you can reduce by paying extra daily insurance. Most companies won't insure you for travel in a two-wheel drive on the many unsealed roads, so check your contract carefully. Major Sydney car-hire firms are:

Avis: *214 William St. Tel: (02) 9357 2000/statewide 1800 22 55 33.*
Budget: *93 William St, Kings Cross. Tel: (02) 9339 8803, statewide 13 27 27, campervans 1800 643 985.*
Hertz: *cnr William and Rilley Sts. Tel: (02) 9360 6621, national 133 039, campervans, 1800 33 58 88.*
Kings Cross Rentals: *169 William St. Tel: (02) 9361 0637/toll free 1800 676 259.*
Thrifty: *75 William St. Tel: (02) 9331 1385.*

Driving rules: Australians drive on the left-hand side, giving way to the right. Speed limits change frequently, so watch for the signs, but generally, it's 60kmh in towns, 100kmh on highways and country roads, and occasionally rising to 110kmh on straight stretches. The police are hot on speeders and drink-drivers – the permitted alcohol level is 0.05 per cent. Seat belts are compulsory, back and front. Overseas driving licences are valid, non-English versions must be accompanied by a translation – keep it with you on all journeys.

CityRail trains

CityRail trains run 0430–2400 daily, connecting Sydney's city centre with the outer suburbs. Central station is the heart of the network, with several lines looping the City Circle – Museum, St James, Circular Quay, Wynyard and Town Hall. Another useful line is the Illawarra line to Bondi Junction via Martin Place and Kings Cross. A return ticket purchased after 0900 on weekdays is up to 45 per cent cheaper.

Coach

Numerous long-distance coaches depart from Eddy Avenue by Sydney's Central station, serving the main towns of NSW and many of the smaller ones too. Operators include **McCafferty's** (*tel: (02) 9212 3433, central reservations 131 499, www.mccaffertys.com.au*), **Greyhound-Pioneer** (*tel: (02) 9212 1500, 24-hour reservations and enquiries, 132 030, www.greyhound. com.au*). A huge variety of passes is available.

Explorer tickets

The hop on, hop off explorer buses are the easiest way to see Sydney. There are two routes to choose from – the red **Sydney Explorer**, which takes in 24 main sights from the Opera House to

Kings Cross and Darling Harbour on a 28km round trip, running at 17-minute intervals. The 19-stop **Bondi & Bay Explorer** follows a 30km coastal route from Circular Quay to Watson's Bay and Bondi. Both depart from Alfred St, Circular Quay – buy the daily ticket on the bus.

Ferries

Sydney's ferries are a cheap way to sightsee from the water and the easiest option for Manly, Taronga Zoo and Watson's Bay. They all depart from Circular Quay, and run from around 0600 to 2400. The **Jetcat** is a quicker

(and pricier) version of the ordinary ferries. **Sydney Ferries** also run harbour cruises that are substantially cheaper than commercial alternatives.

Information

The information line for **Sydney Buses**, **Sydney Ferries** and **CityRail** is *131 500 (0600–2200)*. Bus information kiosks are found at Alfred St (Circular Quay), Queen Victoria Building, Manly Wharf and Bondi Junction. Circular Quay (opposite jetty 5) and Central station (platform 10) have **CityRail** information booths, whilst ferry information (*tel: (02) 9207 3170*) is available opposite wharf 4 at Circular Quay. All can provide the excellent *Sydney Public Transport Map.*

unlimited travel on Sydney Buses and Ferries and the Explorer buses, plus Sydney Ferries cruises, the JetCat and the Central Business District CityRail network.

Monorail and Sydney Light Rail

More an unusual way of sightseeing than a practical mode of transport, the **monorail** is a 3.5km raised scenic loop linking the city centre with all the attractions of Darling Harbour. It runs from around 0700 to 2200, later at weekends. There are ticket machines at all seven stations. **Sydney Light Rail (SLR)** runs to Darling Harbour from Central station.

Taxis

Taxis are relatively inexpensive and plentiful. They are metered and can easily be flagged down in the street. Major companies include **ABC Cabs** (*tel: 132 522*), **Legion Cabs** (*tel: 131 451*), **RSL Cabs** (*tel: 132 211*), **St George Cabs** (*tel: 132 166*).

Passes

Inexpensive **one-day passes** are available for unlimited bus travel, combined bus and ferry travel, combined bus and rail travel (within the central area) and a combination of all three. A weekly **TravelPass**, which allows unlimited travel on CityRail trains, Sydney Buses and Sydney Ferries, is a sound investment for a hectic week's sightseeing. Travel passes are available from CityRail stations, bus kiosks and some newsagents. Visitors to Taronga Zoo, Sydney Aquarium or Manly's Oceanworld can buy passes which include the entry fee and return ferry at a slight saving on normal prices. The **SydneyPass**, available for three, five or seven days, offers

Tours

If you don't plan to hire a car, many of the attractions around Sydney – Port Stephens, Blue Mountains, Hunter Valley – can easily be visited on day excursions. Don't bother with Canberra – it's too rushed in one day. Various excursion operators – **Murrays** (*tel: 132 251*), **Great Sights** (*tel: (02) 9241 2294*) – are based at the Day Tour Terminal, Circular Quay West, with **AAT Kings** (*tel: (02) 9252 2788*) and **ATS** (*tel: (02) 9555 2700*) at jetty 6, Circular Quay.

Outside Sydney

Coff's Harbour: Pete's Picnic at Dorrigo (*tel: (02) 6653 7115*). This fun day out on a 1972 doubledecker bus in the company of the cheeky and charming Pete takes in the craft shops of Bellingen, the rainforest at Dorrigo, Dangar Falls and the Steam and Railway Museum, plus scones and a barbie. The best wildlife tour is to Tidbinbilla near Canberra with **Round About** tours (*tel: (02) 6259 5999*) whilst alternative (backpacker-ish) fun awaits on **Mick's** (*tel: (02) 6685 6889*) and **Jim's** (*tel: (02) 6685 7720*) tours to **Nimbin** via various scenic swimming holes.

Train

CityRail network also includes intercity trains to the Blue Mountains, Newcastle in the north and as far as Goulburn and Nowra in the south. Long-distance and interstate train services are provided by CountryLink, some of which link up to coach services. There are three services a day between Sydney and Canberra, Coffs Harbour, and Grafton, daily services to Byron Bay. *Tel: 132 232 for information, and bookings, which are essential.*

Don't miss

In Sydney . . .

1 The Opera House

With its white shells reaching up into a blue NSW sky, it's as innately Australian as the kangaroo and the koala. The harbourside walk from this unique symbol of Sydney to Mrs Macquarie's Chair is one of the best in the city. **Pages 30-31**

2 The Harbour Bridge

Be sure to walk over it, cycle across, take the train or, better still, climb up to the arch's mid-point for a top-of-the-city view. **Pages 44–45**

3 The Rocks

This 19th-century village combines heritage and history with excellent restaurants, great pubs and souvenirs. **Pages 46–47**

4 Powerhouse Museum

Forget stodgy and staid displays – this vibrant museum puts the fun into the past and present with an interactive kaleidoscope of Australia's social history, triumphs, inventions, transport and more. **Pages 42–43**

5 Paddington

Known to Sydneysiders as 'Paddo', this bohemian suburb houses the city's best examples of wrought-iron colonial 'lacework', as well as independent art galleries, a plethora of coffee shops, quirky fashion boutiques and the wonderful Saturday craft market. **Pages 60-61**

6 Bondi to Coogee coastal walk

It's the ultimate soul-soothing scene – a rugged coastline, clear sky, golden beaches, a profusion of wildflowers and a chance to observe Sydney's city dwellers at play. **Page 73**

And beyond . . .

7 Port Macquarie

A hospital for koalas, a stunning coastal walk and proximity to the atmospheric waterfall and rainforest gorge at Boorganna Nature Reserve make this the perfect haven to enjoy the north coast's natural beauty. **Pages 104–107**

8 Byron Bay

Australia's most easterly town has a year-round holiday atmosphere with great surf, cosmopolitan restaurants, a lively nightlife, alternative experiences and rainforest scenery thrown in. **Pages 120–121**

9 Jervis Bay

North coast fans complain that the south coast waters are much cooler, but that's a small price to pay for unspoilt, dazzling white sands, a prolific parrot population and the stunning sandstone scenery which surrounds this beautiful natural harbour. **Page 138**

10 National Gallery of Australia, Canberra

The many strands of Australia's diverse cultures are reflected here with poignant aboriginal works, early European settlers' paintings and contemporary Australian masterpieces, plus a fair sprinkling of prestigious international works. The sculpture garden on the shore of Lake Burley Griffin is a delight. **Pages 154–155**

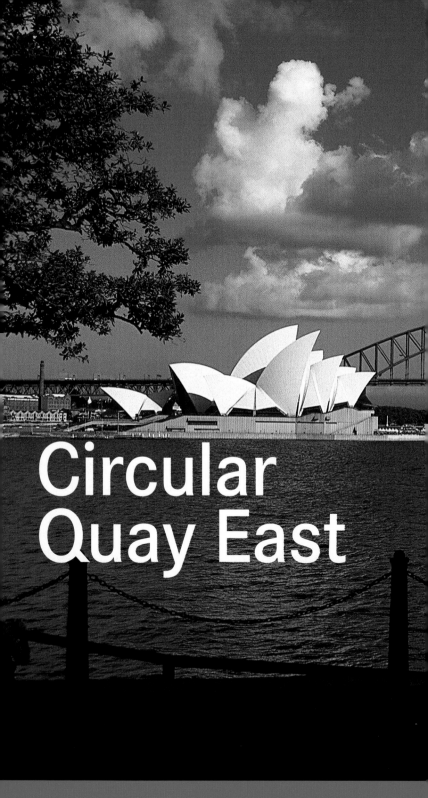

Circular Quay East

Vibrant and buzzing, the area around Circular Quay throngs with goggle-eyed tourists, taking in the splendour of the magnificent opera house, the majestic Harbour Bridge and the sheer beauty of a city built around the water. But if a cool beer at a harbourside café, while watching the buskers and cosmopolitan crowds isn't entertainment enough, stunning gardens, intriguing museums and spectacular colonial buildings are but a short walk away.

CIRCULAR QUAY EAST

Circular Quay East

*Getting there: Circular Quay ferry/station, for waterfront attractions. St James Park station for Domain, Macquarie St. Martin Place station for Art Gallery of NSW, Royal Botanic Gardens. **Sydney Explorer** for all.*

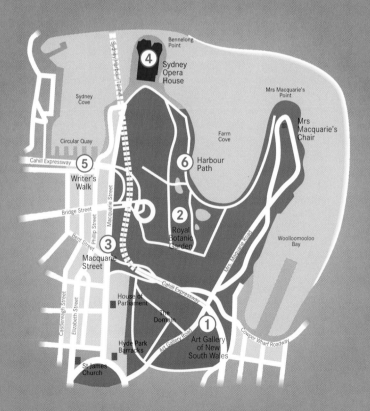

① Artistic treasures

Take a tour of the Art Gallery of New South Wales with one of the wonderfully informative guides. They'll give you an insight into Australia's own brand of impressionism, explain the history behind aboriginal totems with a few Monets and Matisses into the bargain.
Pages 24–26

② Green fingered paradise

See plants so rare they're kept in cages, view tropical blooms in a space age pyramid or indulge your gardening spirit with lunch at the tree-shaded restaurant at the Royal Botanic Garden. **Page 27**

③ Macquarie Street

From St James church to the Hyde Park Barracks, this street is a monument to the works of Francis Greenway, ex-British con turned father of Australian architecture. **Page 28–29**

④ A night at the Opera

Up there with the kangaroo as the internationally recognised symbol of Australia, the Opera House, with its white shells reaching up to the sky, is a unique piece of architecture – and no disappointment when you get up close.
Pages 30–31

⑤ Wise words

It's the equivalent of flicking through a much-loved book of quotations: a stroll around Writers Walk, will allow you a sometimes poignant, sometimes amusing, often historical insight into Australia through the eyes of famous writers and poets. **Page 31**

⑥ Harbourside walk

Soothing to the soul and a balm to the eyes, walk along the harbour path from the Opera House to Mrs Macquarie's Chair. Work will seem a million miles away as you share the wonderful views with couples in love, dawdling tourists and dog walkers. **Page 31**

Art Gallery of New South Wales

Tel: (02) 9225 1744; what's on recorded info line: (02) 9225 1790.
Open daily 1000–1700.

This wonderful gallery is the sort of place you can dip in and out of – it's free, well laid out and knowledgeable volunteers run superb guided tours. Its strength lies in its 19th- and 20th-century Australian collection, with some good European works and an interesting Yiribana gallery of aboriginal and Torres Strait Islander art.

The large **Australian collection** encompasses works from the early 1800s to the mid 20th century, showing the transition from colonial painters entrenched in an English style to the development of techniques capable of rendering the idiosyncrasies of the Australian landscape.

Australian highlights

- There are several excellent examples of **colonial art** in which the artists are strongly influenced by London's painting styles. **Conrad Marten**'s *Wiseman's Ferry* (1838) is a good example of this, as are the works of **John Glover**, who arrived in Australia in 1832. His painting, *Natives on the Ouse River, Van Diemen's Land* (1838) show the clarity of light in the southern hemisphere and the idyllic relationship the aboriginals had with the land until the white settlers interfered.

- Look out for the **9 by 5 paintings**, which formed part of a famous Melbourne exhibition in 1889. They were painted by three artists from the Heidelberg School: **Arthur Streeton**, **Tom Roberts** and **Charles Conder** on cedar cigar-box lids (hence the 9 by 5 tag) and characterised by fresh colours, quickly paced brush strokes and informal compositions.

● Other Australian **Impressionist** paintings worth looking out for are *Fire's on* by Arthur Streeton, *Departure of the SS* Orient – *Circular Quay* by Charles Conder and one of the most famous paintings in Australian art, *Shearing at Newstead (The Golden Fleece)* by Tom Roberts. The latter was a tribute to the men who worked so hard to create an industry and reflects the heat, the dust and sheer effort involved.

● **Frederick McCubbin** was best known for his depiction of the textures of the Australian bush as seen in his painting *On the Wallaby Track* (1896).

● **Rupert Bunny**, **George Lambert** and **Hugh Ramsay** were the stars of the early 20th century, all well known for their ability to paint human figures. Look out for *A Summer Morning* (1908) by Bunny, *Holiday in Essex* (1910) by Lambert and *The Sisters* (1904) by Ramsay.

● More contemporary offerings include **Arthur Boyd**'s *Expulsion* (1947–8), which features Adam and Eve being chased out of the Australian bush, illustrating his penchant for combining biblical subjects with an Australian backdrop.

● **Brett Whiteley** was amongst the most famous of Australian contemporary artists, best known for his match sculpture representing old and new Australia on the edge of the Domain. A great fan of Matisse, he was a very eclectic artist who incorporated the use of space typical of Asian painting into his work. One of his most attractive paintings is the sumptuous *Balcony 2*, a view of Sydney Harbour at night painted from Lavender Bay.

Fleeting moment

Tom Roberts was the first to recognise the possibilities of applying French Impressionist techniques to render the colour and light of the Australian landscape. He introduced the plein air *impressionist technique to his contemporaries, McCubbin, Streeton and Conder, who set out to capture the fleeting moment such as trains arriving and football games in motion.*

● Other 20th-century Australian artists to look out for include **William Dobell**, who is recognised for his 1950s portrait paintings, **Lloyd Rees** for his landscape paintings and **Margaret Preston** for her modern 1920s images.

European highlights

- The imposing *Cymon and Iphigenia* (*c*1884), by Englishman **Frederic Leighton**, is one of the best examples in the gallery of Victorian Olympian style. It depicts the moment that the sight of the sleeping Iphigenia transforms shepherd boy Cymon into an enlightened admirer of beauty and knowledge.

- **Ford Madox Brown**'s *Chaucer at the Court of Edward III* (1847–51), his largest and most ambitious painting, is the gallery's most famous European work. He wanted to pay homage to the great English poet, reminding Australians of the origin of their native tongue.

- **Camille Pissarro**'s *Peasants Houses, Eragny* (1887) is one of the best examples of neo-impressionism in the gallery. Pissarro gained much of his inspiration from the countryside, depicting it as a realm of continuity and timeless values shaped by peasant labour.

- **Pablo Picasso**'s *Nude in a Rocking Chair* (1956) was painted when he was 75. It depicts his future second wife, Jacqueline Roque at his villa in Cannes.

Yiribana gallery

This is a lovely airy gallery on the lower floor. The highlights include the atmospheric **Pukumani** grave posts, in which carved forms and painted motifs represent the transition between life and death. There's also a fine collection of heads painted on sandstone and the *Fruit Bats* by **Lin Onus** – 99 fibreglass fruit bats hanging on a washing line painted with aboriginal designs.

Getting there: Art Gallery Rd. St James Station, Sydney Explorer. Free.

Monet's technique

To create the sense of power of the Atlantic in his painting, Port Goulphar, Belle-Ile *(1887) Monet had himself lashed to the rocks so that he could feel the spray washing over him. He wanted to convey the storm-blasted appearance of the coast, describing it as 'a landscape superb in its savagery, an accumulation of terrible rocks and a sea incredible in its colours'.*

The Royal Botanic Garden

Mrs Macquarie's Rd. Tel: 02 9231 8111. Open 0800–1700 in winter, to 2000 in summer. Visitor's centre (maps, books, self-guide audio tours) open 0930–1630. Guided walks daily at 1030, except public holidays. Martin Place/Circular Quay station, Sydney Explorer, Bus 438. Free except for Tropical Centre.

The exceptional views and beautiful walks are reason enough to visit these gardens, although keen gardeners will fizz over the variety of 7500 plants, some so rare they have to be locked in a cage. The gardens are also the idyllic setting for a series of evening classical concerts around the end of November, beginning of December. The best way to explore is on foot, but a trackless train with a commentary runs every 15 minutes from the visitor's centre. The **Tropical centre** (*open daily 1000–1600; $*) is a glasshouse pyramid where you can see native plants from mountains and rainforests. The neighbouring glass arc houses non-native exotic species.

The nearby **Fernery** (*open daily 1000–1600*) is home to subtropical, warm and cool temperate climate ferns from all over the world, whilst a stroll through the shady **Palm Grove** takes in over 180 species, the rarest palm collection in the world. The central lake supports a variety of birdlife including the native Australian ibis bird, which nests in the tops of the palm trees.

Wollemi pine

The Wollemi pine is so rare, it has to be kept in a cage as it's one of only 38 trees known in the wild. It was thought to be extinct until 1994, when it was discovered in an almost impenetrable sandstone gorge in Wollemi National Park, 150km northwest of Sydney.

Macquarie St

Named after Governor Lachlan Macquarie, Macquarie St is the most prestigious address in Sydney, home to leading medical specialists and many fine colonial buildings.

The Domain

Macquarie St. St James/Martin Place stations, Bus 200. Buses 380, 382, 390–2, 394, 396–9 run parallel in Elizabeth St. Open 24 hours.

Established in 1788 by Governor Phillip as a park for the governor and the crown, it contained the first farm in Australia. Nowadays it's a chilling-out area for people reading their books and papers or simply enjoying the sun. The normally peaceful atmosphere is transformed on Sundays, when the soap boxes line the main thoroughfare *à la* London Speakers' Corner and the passionate, pleading and just plain potty have their say on God, vegetarianism, the uselessness of men and the dangers of alcohol. During the January **Sydney Festival**, it's home to free jazz, opera and classical music concerts.

House of Parliament

Macquarie St. Open Mon–Fri, 0930–1600. Free guided tours run at 1000, 1100 and 1400.

The magnificent colonnaded building (1816) which houses the legislative assemblies of New South Wales was once a wing of the neighbouring convict-built Sydney Hospital, known as the 'Rum Hospital' because it was built on the proceeds of rum importation and resale. A visit here is amazingly informal and a guided tour will help you appreciate the building and understand the intricacies of state government. If Parliament is in session, you might catch some of the combative question time.

The highlight of the building is the spectacular book-lined **Jubilee Room**, built in 1905 as the main reading room of the Parliamentary Library. It has an ornate stained-glass window, as well as displays and photos tracing the history of the building and Parliament since 1770. In the front lobby are the opal-encrusted scissors used by **Jack Lang**, the Premier of New South Wales, to cut the ribbon on the opening of Sydney Harbour Bridge in 1932 (*see pages 44–45*).

Hyde Park Barracks

Queen's Square, Macquarie St. Open daily 0930–1700. $$.

Designed by the convict architect, **Francis Greenway**, these beautiful buildings are considered to be amongst his finest work. Originally conceived and used as convict barracks from 1819–48, the building housed an immigration depot for women during the latter half of the 19th century, and then courts and legal offices. Refurbished in 1990, Hyde Park Barracks is now a museum about itself, unravelling the story of the various occupants who used it over 180 years.

Many of the text-heavy displays take a bit of ploughing through, although there are interesting personal histories of women who emigrated to the colony from Britain and Ireland to balance the male population. There's a fascinating display of material discovered under the floorboards during renovation in the 1980s. Upstairs is a convict dormitory with hammocks you can try out, plus a convict database.

St James Church

173 King St. Open daily 0900–1700. Free.

Another Greenway gem, this simple, graceful building is the city's oldest church, consecrated in 1824. It was originally designed as a courthouse, before plans to build a cathedral on George St were scuppered. The stained-glass windows are mainly modern, representing the elements of earth, air, fire and water.

Sydney Opera House

Bennelong Point, Circular Quay station, then walk east along the harbour, Sydney Explorer, Bus 438. Box Office: Open Mon–Sat, 0900–2030. Hour-long guided tours of the theatres and foyers run continuously between 0900 and 1600, from the lower concourse. $$.

Billed as the eighth wonder of the world, this unique building is the internationally recognised symbol of Sydney. It was designed by a Danish architect, **Jorn Utzon**, who beat off the opposition from 233 contenders in the 1957 design competition. An appeal was set up to provide the required funds, but when lacklustre response raised only $900,000, the Australian lottery was set up to cover the estimated $7 million needed.

Unhappy architects

Building started in 1959, yet the complexity of the design and resulting engineering problems meant that the building took 14 years to build and costs spiralled to a final total of $102 million. Utzon stormed away from the project in 1966 over a disagreement over his fees and preferred suppliers. Consequently, when the building opened in 1973, the grandeur of the outside with its 'shells' covered in over a million tiny tiles outshone the less imaginative interior.

Modern-day theatre

However, as one of the busiest performing art centres in the world, the Opera House serves its purpose well, hosting around 3000 events a year for 2 million visitors. It's a labyrinth of nearly 1000 rooms comprising 60 dressing rooms and 5 rehearsal studios as well as eating areas, offices and the machinery rooms necessary to keep the well-oiled wheels of the Opera House running. The Opera House is actually a

Tip

misnomer – events include all manner of performing arts from dance, music and pop concerts to variety shows, ballet and plays. There are five main theatres – the largest, the **Concert Hall**, with seating for over 2600 people, has excellent acoustics and lends itself to musical events. The **Opera Theatre**, under the largest 'shell', tends to show performances of ballet, dance and, of course, opera. The newest performing space, **The Studio**, was opened in 1999 for the production of experimental and contemporary arts such as comedy, jazz, techno, dance and cabaret.

Writers Walk

Writers Walk runs from just beyond the Opera House right round to the Rocks. A series of plaques set in the pavement encase the wise, witty and often profound words of writers. They include quotations from Australian wordsmiths such as Clive James as well as international writers (such as D H Lawrence) who have visited Australia.

Harbourside walk

A spectacular harbourside walk runs from the Opera House, through the Royal Botanic Garden, around Farm Cove, to the carved waterfront seat known as **Mrs Macquarie's Chair**. The Governor Macquarie had a road built down to this point in 1816 so that his wife had better access to her favourite views.

In the wings

For a first-hand insight to how the scenery rises up from under the stage in the Opera Theatre or the light and sound booths operate in the Drama Theatre, the Opera House's backstage tours whisk you up and down 300 steps into areas not usually accessible to the public. Commentary is peppered with amusing anecdotes about performing gaffes, with glimpses of the rehearsals of prestigious productions into the bargain. Tours (for ages 12-plus) run on selected mornings depending on who is rehearsing what. Tel: (02) 9250 7250 for information. $$$.

Restaurants

Art Gallery Café
Art Gallery of NSW, Art Gallery Rd.
Open daily 0900–1700. $. This
reasonably priced café serves dainty
light lunches on a beautiful flower-
filled terrace overlooking Sydney.
It's a lovely place to linger over a
book or newspaper.

Bennelong Restaurant
Sydney Opera House. Tel: (02) 9250
7545. Open Mon–Fri 1200–2330,
Sat 1030–2330, Sun 1030–1600.
$$$. Dinner in this posh but pleasant
glass-encased restaurant is a little like
having dinner in a goldfish bowl, and
appropriately, it's a haven for fish fans
with all manner of shellfish, oysters
and lobsters. There's a formal dining
area, plus a crustacean and cocktail bar.

Botanic Gardens Restaurant
Royal Botanic Gardens. Open daily
for lunch. Tel: (02) 9241 2419. $$$.
There's no better antidote to Stendhal's
syndrome than a lazy lunch on the
shady upstairs veranda here. Delicacies
include smoked salmon with crisp
salads, steamed chicken with spicy
lentils and some mouth-watering
desserts. The informal café downstairs
serves snacks, cake and coffee.

Concourse restaurant
Sydney Opera House. Tel: (02) 9250
7300. Open Mon–Sat 1000–2030, Sun
1000–1700. No bookings 1700–2000.
$$. On the plus side, the food ranges
from quick snack sandwiches to fresh
fish and fancy pasta served at a speed
to get you to the theatre on time. On
the minus, its lower parade position
means those great views over the
harbour are out of eyeshot.

Pavillion on the Park
1 Art Gallery Rd. Tel: (02) 9232 1322.
Café open 0900–1700; $$. Restaurant,
lunch Sun–Fri, dinner Thur–Sat, $$$.
The pleasant outdoor café serves
delicious brunch-style food all day –
buttermilk pancakes with ricotta and
bananas, mushroom and cheese risotto
– plus wonderful coffee and cakes. The
excellent restaurant alongside is floor-
to-ceiling glass with a view over the
Domain, serving modern Australian
dishes (sea scallops with green papaya,
marinated quail breast) with flair.

Sydney Cove Oyster Bar
Circular Quay East. Open daily
1200–2000 winter, to 2300 summer.
$$$. If the budget is tight, order a light
meal of cheese and fruit, or hang it all
and indulge in a half lobster and bottle
of chilled wine. But spend some time
here – it's not cheap, but then the
location is priceless.

What to try

How do pie, peas and chilli dogs sound
as a late-night snack when you've been
on the booze? It sounds bizarre, but
those in the know head to the Sydney
institution, **Harry's Café de Wheels**
(*Cowper's Wharf Rd, Woolloomooloo*
Bay), where Harry has been serving
the drunk and the famous from his
take-away van since 1945. Open 0730
until the wee hours, it's plastered with
pics of celebrities who've joined his
colourful clientele.

CIRCULAR QUAY EAST

The Harbour

Sydney's natural harbour is one of the most glorious in the world. It's the soul of Sydney, creating a feeling of countryside, space and freedom right at the heart of the city.

Its 52 square kilometres of water stretch from the mouth of the Parramatta River to the entrance of the Tasman Sea, framed by rocky headlands at the North and South Heads. The indented coastline is studded with beautiful coves and secluded bays, doubling up as the city's playground with swimming, wind surfing, yachting and an armada of pleasure cruises. It's the top spot for watching the annual **firework bonanza** around the Harbour Bridge on New Year's Eve and the starting-point for the fiercely competitive annual **Sydney to Hobart (Tasmania) race,** which leaves from Rushcutter's Bay on Boxing Day. But most of all, Sydney's waterways allow Sydney's true beach bums a wonderful quality of life. The vital ferry transport links enable the surfing set to work in the centre and live by the sea.

Given the spectacular views, it comes as no surprise that the most **prestigious properties** cluster around the harbour shores. Areas such as Point Piper, Double Bay and Rose Bay on the south shore and Kirribilli and Mosman on the north shore boast stunning waterfront dwellings, sophisticated combinations of balconies, huge windows and harbourside

CIRCULAR QUAY EAST

Prestigious homes

So prized are Sydney's harbour views that no one ever dreamed that developers would manage to secure planning permission for a luxury apartment block just along from the Opera House on East Circular Quay. Amidst huge outrage and controversy, the $750 million, 237-apartment project was given the go-ahead in the mid 1990s, with two-bedroom apartments in the first stage of the development currently on sale for a whacking $1.5 million.

terraces. Double Bay panders to its wealthy inhabitants with a distinctly designer shopping area, whilst Rose Bay is home to the exclusive Royal Sydney Golf Club, which has a 20-year waiting list. It's no coincidence that the sea-plane service to Palm Beach operates from here.

The harbour is dotted with tiny islands, of which the best known is **'Pinchgut' Island**, so called because Captain Phillip dumped prisoners here for a week with very meagre rations in the colony's early days. In 1796, convicted murderer Francis Morgan was hanged in chains, with his body left to rot for three years as an *aide-mémoire* to potentially disobedient convicts. The tiny **Fort Denison** was built in the 1850s to protect the city from the distant threat of invasion after the discovery of gold, but a shot has never been fired in anger.

CIRCULAR QUAY EAST

Circular
Quay West

The Rocks and Darling Harbour are separated by 200 years of history, their respective importance in city life at the opposite ends of the spectrum: the ultra historical and mega modern. The Rocks, the birthplace of Australia in 1788, is a place for soaking up history, where every corner, every cobblestone tells the story of the transition from a lawless colony of felons to modern-day elegance and prosperity. Darling Harbour winds the clock forward to 1988, when a host of exciting tourist attractions – the Aquarium, the Maritime Museum, the Powerhouse – came into being.

Sydney Aquarium

NEW GREAT BARRIER REEF
COMPLEX NOW OPEN
ENTRANCE 100m →

CIRCULAR QUAY WEST

BEST OF
Circular
Quay West

Getting there: **Darling Harbour:** *Monorail/Sydney Light Rail (SLR): Harbourside monorail, Pyrmont Bay SLR for the Maritime Museum, Haymarket for Powerhouse Museum and Paddy's Market. Walk from Town Hall Station. Bus 456/888. Sydney Explorer.* **The Rocks:** *Walk west from Circular Quay station/ferry, Sydney Explorer. Come Saturday or Sunday for the colourful George St craft market (1000–1700) and street entertainment.*

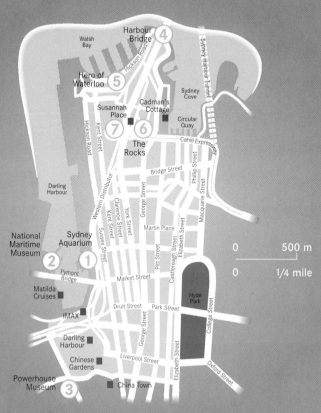

① *Fishy tales*

The Sydney Aquarium is simply splendid – an accessible, fascinating display of all that lurks in the underwater world surrounding Australia's coasts. View the nasty Old Wife with dorsal spines which inject painful poisons into puncture wounds, or admire the beautiful striped Emperor Angelfish, all to a background of *Jaws*-like music. **Page 40**

② *Sail away*

One of the most striking things about Sydney is the major role that the sea plays in city life – from the leisure pursuits of the city beaches to the sea trade, which has built up commercial fortunes over the last 200 years. The National Maritime Museum reels in all this and more, with plenty of opportunity simply to admire sea-going vessels past and present. **Page 42**

③ *Power to the people*

There's no deathly hush at the Powerhouse Museum, no quiet tiptoeing about between exhibits. The emphasis at this treasure trove of industrial, scientific and social history is on fun . . . climb up onto steam locomotives, watch a 100-year-old steam engine crank into action, plan your own Apollo space shuttle expedition. **Pages 42–43**

④ *Feel the fear and do it anyway*

Sydney is a city of panoramas over sandy bays, views from craggy headlands, vistas over spectacular buildings that punctuate the skyline. Roll them all up into one with an adrenalin-pumping climb to the top of Harbour Bridge – it's not just a tourist attraction, it's a privilege. **Pages 44–45**

⑤ *Have a beer*

Check out the historical **Hero of Waterloo Hotel**, a beautiful corner building where press-gangs plied men with ale then marched them onto ships through tunnels leading from the cellars to the wharf. Today, it's a good drinking pub without whaling ships waiting for you at the other end. **Page 47**

⑥ *Rock on*

Get a feel for life in New South Wales as a fledgling colony with a walking tour through the sandstone streets of the Rocks. Explore the higgledy-piggledy maze of huge 19th-century warehouses, narrow alleys where press-gangs prowled and central precincts where makeshift hospitals tried to nurse ailing convicts back to health. **Pages 46–47**

⑦ *Shopping*

From the weekend market of bric-à-brac, recycled art and trendy souvenirs to the upmarket opal shops and the chic of the Argyle stores, the Rocks is a colourful shopping area of contemporary designs and one-off craft boutiques. **Page 49**

Tourist information

Darling Harbour Visitor's Information Centre: between the Imax Theatre and SegaWorld. *Tel: 9286 0111.*

39

China Town

Monorail/SLR: Haymarket, Central station – walk down George St and Hay St.

A bustling area of herbalists, ethnic shops, exotic greengrocers and oriental restaurants – and **Paddy's market**, one of the most famous markets in Sydney (*open Sat–Sun 0900–1630*). Here, the Chinese community shop at stalls of shiny, sun-ripened fruit and veg, whilst sun-hatted tourists sift through the mêlée of cheap T-shirts, pet rabbits and canaries, kangaroo skins, boomerangs, jewellery, tropical fish and tacky souvenirs.

Darling Harbour

Town Hall station. Monorail/SLR: Haymarket, Convention, Harbourside. Sydney Explorer. Bus 456/888.

Extensive redevelopment in the 1980's transformed this once-run-down area of disused docks and railway yards into Darling Harbour, a lively waterfront playground with colourful street performers and huge water features for people to paddle and play in. Some of Sydney's best tourist attractions are here: the **Aquarium**, **Powerhouse** and the **National Maritime Museum**, plus a pleasing array of people-watching restaurants. The **People Mover**, a trackless toy-town-like train, departs every five minutes (*1000–1700*) for a 20-minute harbour tour. There are stops, but signal the train for a swift pick-up.

Sydney Aquarium

Open daily 0930–2200. $$. Monorail: Darling Park, Sydney Explorer, walk from city centre down Market St/King St, Ferry/charter boat to Aquarium Pier, Town Hall station.

Fascinating displays of all that's weird and wonderful in the world beneath the sea combine with hands-on rock pools and underwater walkways to make this an exciting trip for any age. The newest oceanarium, **Jewels of the Great Barrier Reef**, which allows you to stand nose (to glass) to nose with sharks, sting rays, sea turtles and a host of brightly coloured tropical fish is spectacular, but check out the **Sydney Harbour Oceanarium**, seal sanctuary and crocodile pool too.

Chinese Gardens

Open daily 0930–1830. Tea House open 1000–1730. $. Monorail/SLR: Haymarket, Sydney Explorer, Central station – walk down Hay St and Harbour St.

If you want to escape the madding crowds, seek out this peaceful oasis of waterfalls, lakes and shady seats. A labyrinth of pathways weaves past Chinese pavilions, finishing up at the pretty tea house with a veranda overlooking the **Lotus Pond**.

IMAX Cinema

Films are shown daily on the hour, every hour, 1000–2200. Tel: (02) 9281 3300 for programme details. $$. Walk from Town Hall, monorail/SLR: Convention.

The IMAX shows nature and action documentary-type films from around the world in 3-D (with the aid of liquid crystal glasses). For the foot-weary, films such as *Africa's Elephant Kingdom*, *The First City in Space* or *Everest* shown on screens ten times the normal size offer an opportunity to sit down in style.

Matilda Cruises

Harbourside and Aquarium Wharf. Tel: (02) 9264 7377. $$. Monorail/SLR: Convention for harbourside departures, Darling Park monorail or ferry to Aquarium Wharf.

Take a one-hour express tour of Sydney Harbour, with optional stops at the Rocks, the Opera House and Sydney Aquarium. Boats depart from the Harbourside Shopping Centre (and the other embarkation points) eight times daily. The circuit takes one hour if you don't get off, although you can take a whole day to complete the tour, stopping off at all the points on the way.

National Maritime Museum

Open daily 0930–1700. Tel: (02) 9552 7777. $$. SLR: Pyrmont Bay, Monorail: Harbourside, Sydney Explorer, Bus 456.

This indoor and outdoor museum isn't just for maritime buffs. It gives an insight into how the sea has shaped life in Australia. The leisure gallery examines aspects of Aussie beach culture, with quirky exhibitions about the 1930s seaside battles over skimpy swimsuits, alongside boats which have made history such as Ken Warby's *Spirit of Australia*. It broke the world speed record in 1977 and again in 1978 and still stands at 511.11kmh.

The **Passenger** exhibition recalls the experiences of people who made the journey to Australia by sea, in luxury, as penniless immigrants and as desperate refugees. Voice recordings, diary snippets, personal mementoes, letters and clothing evoke the courageous – and sad – adventures of travellers from the convict era to the Indo-Chinese boat people of modern times.

Outside you can climb aboard the HMAS *Vampire*, the Daring class destroyer which served in the Royal Australian Navy 1959–86. It's affectionately known as 'the Bat', and you can explore the captain's room, control room, sick bay and decks.

The Powerhouse Museum

Harris St. Tel: (02) 9217 0111. Open daily 1000–1700. $$. Free highlight tours daily at 1330 (also 1115 at weekends), book at the counter on level 4. Haymarket Monorail/SLR, Sydney Explorer, Bus 501.

This interactive museum housed in a former power station is positively uplifting. It's a genuine something-for-everybody museum, an eclectic mix of social history with transport, technology and decorative arts thrown in.

Level 2

Transport. This houses all modes of getting around from the humble penny farthing, a 1750s sedan chair from London and the magnificent 1928 Bugatti motor car, to the full-size Catalina flying boat, Bleriot monoplane and an 1880s Sydney Hansom cab.

Space. There's the external casing of a Vulcan rocket, which sent Apollo to the moon, a spacesuit worn by the Apollo 13 team and a replica space shuttle to explore.

Level 3

Kings Cinema. This cinema was built to look like an original 1930s art-deco theatre from the Kings Cinema chain. The foyer area includes interior fittings from Sydney's architectural gem, the Queen Victoria Building and seats from the Manly Odeon, which was demolished in 1985.

Level 4

Success and innovation. Interactive displays featuring Australian award-winning designs range from the frivolous to the essential – mechanical legs demonstrating stay-up socks, the first collapsible baby stroller, automated sheep shears and the 'black box' flight data recorder.

Locomotive No 1. Built in England in 1854 by Robert Stephenson, this engine pulled the first passenger train into Sydney a year later. Also check out the ornate carriage built in 1891 to carry the NSW Governor between Government House and his country residence.

Boulton & Watt steam engine. This is the oldest surviving rotative steam engine in the world. It dates from 1784 and worked the malt grinder at the Whitbread Brewery in London for over 100 years, the first machine to replace people in industry. Regular demonstrations throughout the day.

Strasbourg Clock. This hugely ornate astronomical clock was built in 1888 by an eccentric Sydney technician, Richard Smith, to mark the centenary of European settlement. On the hour, a procession of tiny dolls acts out scenes from the Bible, whilst elsewhere other dials and elements whirr into place.

Australian Explorer Helicopter. It was in this small helicopter that Australian explorer, Dick Smith, became the first person to fly solo around the world in a helicopter in 1983.

Sydney 2000

Darling Harbour is a major Olympic venue for the Sydney 2000 games. Wrestling and boxing will take place in the harbourside Exhibition Centre, weightlifting in the Convention Centre and volleyball in the Entertainment Centre.

The Harbour Bridge

Circular Quay ferry and station.

Second only to the Opera House as the symbol of Sydney, this 503m-long single arch bridge, 'the coathanger', is an integral part of the city's landscape.

The building of the Harbour Bridge provided so many jobs in Sydney during 1923–32 that it was known as the **Iron Lung**. Sixteen people died during its construction – and nine of those were minding their own business on the ground. It provided a welcome alternative to ferry rides and long detours to reach the north shore and today supports eight traffic lanes, bicycle paths and railway lines.

CIRCULAR QUAY WEST

The BridgeClimb

5 Cumberland Place, The Rocks. Tel: (02) 9252 0077. Tours daily every 20 minutes. Night climbs run Thur–Sat. $$$.

It took Paul Cave, Chairman of BridgeClimb, six years and $12 million to overcome all the objections to allowing people to climb to the top of the harbour bridge. The climb was finally given the go-ahead in October 1998. A harness and a special bridge suit ensure that the three-hour experience is slick and safe. The climb is a mixture of knee-trembling vertigo and total exhilaration – the least scary part is standing on the very top! The breathtaking views, as far as the Blue Mountains in the west, enable you to see how the Sydney suburb jigsaw slots into place.

In ribbons

Amidst much pomp and ceremony, Jack Lang, Premier of New South Wales was supposed to cut the ribbon to mark the official opening of the Harbour Bridge. However, ardent royalist Francis de Groot galloped up on his horse and slashed the ribbon with his sword in protest because a member of the royal family hadn't been invited to do the honours.

CIRCULAR QUAY WEST

The Rocks

This is where the First Fleet set foot on Australian soil, way back in 1788, when the shores were home to aborigines. Today, it's a lively, vibrant area, a beautifully preserved 19th-century village with a labyrinth of streets lined with old sandstone warehouses, historical buildings, colonial hotels and pubs, as well as interesting one-off shops and gourmet restaurants.

Start at **Cadman's Cottage** (1816), at 110 George St, the oldest house in Sydney. It was originally a waterfront cottage for the government's coxswain, although land down to the water has been reclaimed since then. Next door is the **Visitor's Centre**, the main information centre for Sydney and NSW, originally the Sydney Sailors' Home designed to provide cheap, safe accommodation for visiting sailors. Carry straight on, detouring off to the right to **Campbell's Cove**, where you can either sit on the steps and admire the view or indulge at one of the excellent waterfront restaurants housed in **Campbell's storehouses**, beautiful sandstone buildings dating from 1839. They originally housed tea, sugar and cloth imported from India and you can still see the pulleys which hauled the cargo up from the docks.

Return to George St and walk under the bridge pylons to **Lower Fort St**, an attractive road lined with lacework houses. Turn left and walk to the corner of Windmill St, where you can refresh yourself at the **Hero of Waterloo Hotel**, a favourite drinking hole since 1844. Underneath it is a cellar, where men more than a little worse for wear would be taken and led to the docks through connecting underground tunnels as extra hands for the ships. At the end of Lower Fort St is the **Garrison Church**, the first military church in Australia, built in 1840 and enlarged by architect Edmund Blacket 15 years later. Here you can either take a right turn to Argyle Place, Sydney's only village green, and stop for a beer at the oldest pub in the city, the **Lord Nelson Hotel** (1842) on Kent St, before continuing up to **Observatory Hill** for a spectacular view over the Rocks. Or you can head back to the village's centre by turning left through the **Argyle Cut**, hacked out of the sandstone by convicts over a 24-year period from 1843. Turn right into Harrington St, where a flight of steps leads up to the historic houses of **Susannah Place** in Gloucester St (*see below*). The Missionary steps lead down to **Nurses Walk** where the first makeshift hospitals were set up. At the far end is one of the narrowest streets in the area, **Suez Canal**, which used to be an open sewer running down to the harbour. From here, you can head back to George St and visit the **Museum of Contemporary Art**, which hosts exhibitions and houses works by 20th-century artists including Warhol, Hockney and Lichtenstein (*tel: (02) 9241 5892; open daily 1000–1800; $$*).

Best Rocks Tour

Tue, Thur–Sun, departing 1830; tel: (02) 9555 2700. $$.
History, Convicts and Murder Most Foul . . . Dressed as a pirate and wielding a cat o'nine tails, ball and chain and lantern, Chris O'Neill walks the Rocks, combining a love of storytelling and drama with factual detail. Tours last 1½ hours, ending up in the Hero of Waterloo for the finale and a free drink.

Susannah Place

58–64 Gloucester St. Open Sat–Sun 1000–1700. $. Circular Quay station/ferry, Explorer Bus.

This row of 1840s working-class terraced houses belonged to Irish immigrants, Edward and Mary Riley. They ran the corner shop, renting out the other houses for £26 per year to fellow immigrants. Now a house museum, the buildings are a mixture of decorative styles reflecting the different eras of occupancy, with recordings from ex-residents recalling life there.

Eating out

Circular Quay west offers quality dining in restaurants along the waterfront or tucked away in the cobbled alleys of the Rocks. New on the gourmet's A–Z is the recently built complex at Cockle Bay Wharf, the latest 'in' place for Sydney's body beautifuls to hang out for dinner with harbourside views.

Cockle Bay Wharf

Darling Park monorail, Town Hall station.

Chinta Ria

The roof terrace. Tel: (02) 9264 3211. Open daily lunch and dinner. $$$. Piquant Malaysian cuisine in an atmospheric Temple of Love, to a background of funky live music and jazz.

Coast

The roof terrace. Tel: (02) 9267 6700. Open daily lunch and dinner. $$$. Contemporary Australian cuisine with an Italian influence.

Pontoon

The promenade. Open daily 1000–late. $$. This bar fits perfectly into the upbeat atmosphere of Cockle Bay with its steel benches, space age pool table and long metal bar serving a crowd of 30-somethings. Small selection of sandwich snacks.

The Rocks

The historical Campbell's Storehouses house an array of superb waterfront restaurants (*all* $$$). Book for outside tables. Choose from Chinese at **The Imperial Harbourside** (*tel: (02) 9247 7073*), seafood at **Waterfront Restaurant** (*tel: (02) 9247 3666*), modern Australian with bush flavours at **Wolfie's Grill** (*tel: (02) 9241 5577*) and Italian at the **Italian Village** (*tel: (02) 9247 6111*).

Elsewhere in the Rocks

Argyle Stores Café

Playfair St. Open daily 1000–1800. $. Classy sandwiches, wonderful coffee and a great array of cakes.

Belmondo's

Gloucester Walk (or through Argyle stores). Tel: (02) 9241 3700. Open lunch Mon–Fri 1200–1430; dinner daily 1830 –2230. $$$. Seriously smart Italian food, although for a fraction of restaurant prices, you can enjoy a plate of antipasti at the bar.

The Harbour Rocks Hotel

34–52 Harrington St. Tel: (02) 9251 8944. $$. Dine on modern Australian fare on the lovely terrace overlooking Nurses Walk. Live jazz on Fridays 1700–2100.

Philip's Foote

101 George St. Tel: (02) 9241 1485. Open daily lunch and dinner. $$. Dinner here is do-it-yourself – pile on the salad, then pick your prime cut and head off to the communal barbecue.

The Wharf

Pier 4, Hickson Road. Tel: (02) 9250 1761. Open Mon–Sat 1200–1500, 1800 onwards. $$$. Sharing the pier with the Sydney Theatre Company, the clientele is colourful and arty, the food Mediterranean biased. You can eat cheaply with an antipasto plate at the bar or have a drink on the big terrace overlooking the harbour ($$).

Darling Harbour and around

Casa Asturiana

77 Liverpool St. Tel: (02) 9264 1010. Open Tue–Fri and Sun for lunch, daily for dinner. $$. A stone's throw from Darling Harbour in the hub of the Spanish quarter, this lively restaurant serves tasty tapas with huge jugs of sangria. Book at weekends.

Powerhouse Garden Restaurant

Powerhouse Museum. Tel: (02) 9217 0559. Open daily 1130–1500. $$. Brightly decorated courtesy of Sydney artist Ken Done, it serves chargrilled octopus, bruschetta and the like plus a fine array of cakes.

Wockpool

Imax Theatre, Darling Harbour. Tel: (02) 9211 9888. Open daily 1200–1500, Sun–Thur 1800–2200, until 2300 Fri–Sat. $$$. Fabulous views and artistically presented modern Asian dishes ranging from deep-fried bug tail won tons to fragrant green fish curry.

Kam Fook Sharks Fin Seafood Restaurant

Level 3, Market City. Tel: (02) 9211 8988/8388. Open Mon–Fri 1000–2300, Sat–Sun 0900–2400. $$. Indulge in Cantonese yum cha – dim sum, braised chicken feet, pork and shrimp won ton and other delicacies, wheeled round to your table on trollies.

Boozing and bands

The Rocks is home to many British-style pubs bearing colonial names such as the **Lord Nelson** (*cnr Kent and Argyle Sts*) and the **Hero of Waterloo** (*81 Lower Fort St*), plus the George St pubs: the **Mercantile Hotel**, the **Fortune of War** and the **Orient**. Most pubs in the Rocks have live bands on Sunday afternoons, and often on Friday and Saturday nights. **The Entertainment Centre** (*Harbour St, Haymarket; tel: (02) 9320 4200, tickets (02) 9266 4800*) hosts massive pop group concerts and big-name rock bands, plus sporting events from wrestling to basketball.

49

Shopping

The Rocks is famed for its opals and souvenir shops – try **Designed and Made: Contemporary Arts and Crafts** (*cnr George St and Playfair St*) and **Australian Craftworks** (*127 George St*) for contemporary ceramics and arty souvenirs, **Argyle stores** (*18–24 Argyle St*) for designer accessories and clothing, **Flame Opals** (*119 George St*) for unset or mounted gems. For a bargain, head to level two at **Market City** for big-name factory outlets.

In the beginning

*When you sit on Campbell's Cove at the Rocks opposite the Opera House, watching the ferries weave in and out of Circular Quay, it's hard to imagine that just over 200 years ago, the whole area was bushland, populated by indigenous tribes. However, the aboriginals' harmonious existence with the land came to an abrupt end in 1788, 18 years after Australia's east coast had been discovered by **Captain Cook**. With convict transportation to America halted by the War of Independence, Britain decided the solution to its overcrowded gaols lay in establishing a far-flung penal colony.*

In 1788, the First Fleet, under the command of **Captain General Phillip**, landed at Sydney Cove with 736 convicts, and around 200 marines. The captain, impressed by the deep harbour and good water supply, described Sydney Cove as 'a noble and capacious harbour, equal, if not superior to any known in the world'. The convicts were quickly put to work clearing land for tents, and later, hacking through the sandstone to create roads. Other convict fleets followed in 1790–1. Many prisoners died *en route*, although conditions for arriving survivors were grim. Food rations were small and famine was a constant threat, as the unskilled workforce struggled to grow food on unfamiliar soils, dogged by a poor water supply and rampant disease.

Under the vision of **Governor Macquarie** (1810–21), the colony began to prosper, particularly after a way was found through the Blue Mountains in 1813 to the fertile hinterland beyond. The Rocks remained the colony's commercial centre, but it was also a lawless area of drunken brawls, whores

and inns of ill-repute. When the young men disappeared to make their fortunes after the discovery of gold in 1850, press-gangs roamed the streets, plying men with drink before forcing them onto the short-staffed whaling ships. The 1870–80s were characterised by violent gang warfare.

Rats!

The turn of the century coincided with an outbreak of bubonic plague, when the government demolished slum housing and burnt many buildings around the harbour to rid the area of rats. Many of the beautiful sandstone buildings and warehouses were earmarked for demolition again in the 1970s to make way for offices, hotels and high-rise housing. The inhabitants formed a vocal protest group, enlisting the help of the **Builders' Labourers' Federation** who imposed a 'green ban' on all demolition and construction work in the area, which forced the authorities to accept a plan for preservation.

The Holey dollar

Governor Macquarie tried to alleviate the shortage of currency that led to the convicts being paid in rum by importing Spanish dollars from India. To stop the exportation of these coins, the centrepiece (the Dump) was cut out, worth about 15 pence, whilst the remainder, the Holey dollar was worth 25 pence.

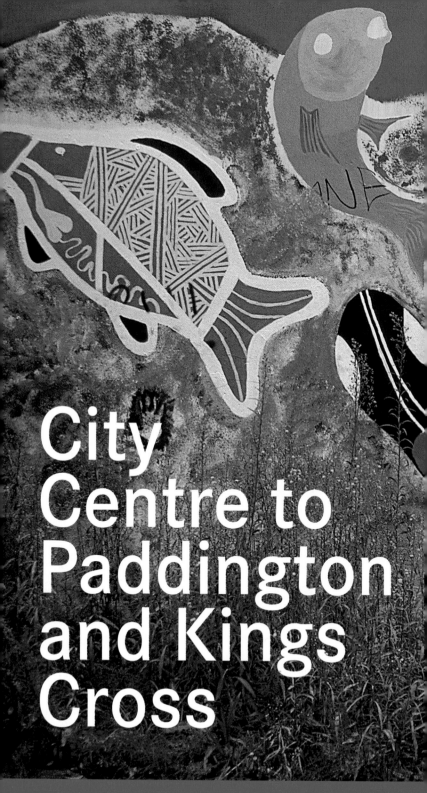

City Centre to Paddington and Kings Cross

A trip from Sydney's centre towards the eastern suburbs encompasses a kaleidoscope of cultures. Slip from the business-like to the bohemian, from the serious-suited Central Business District to the arty, laid-back café culture area of Paddington, and on again to the raunchy, vibrant Kings Cross brimming with nightlife, restaurants, and eccentric characters.

CITY CENTRE TO PADDINGTON AND KINGS CROSS

BEST OF
City Centre to Paddington and Kings Cross

Getting there: **City Centre:** *St James/Martin Place/Town Hall stations, most buses.* **Paddington and Oxford St:** *Buses 378, 380, 382, L82.* **Kings Cross:** *Kings Cross station, Buses 311, 333.* **Sydney Explorer** *for all.*

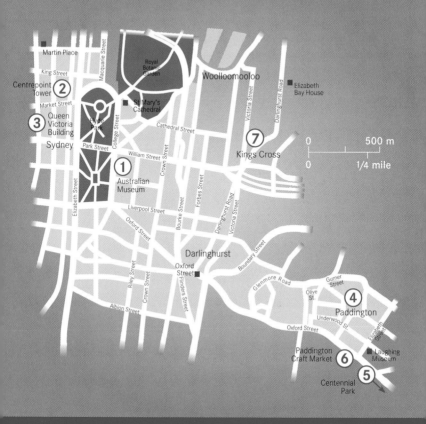

① Fraternise with the dinosaurs

A mixture of awesome and awful, the Australian Museum has some fascinating exhibits to send shivers down your spine. Take the opportunity to view a marine predator 110 million years old and examine the dangerous funnel web spider without leaping on a chair. **Pages 56–57**

② Take a 360-degree tour

Go up to the top of Sydney's highest building, the Centrepoint Tower for lunch in the revolving restaurant with panoramic views. **Page 58**

③ Shop like a queen

Even if you'd rather swim with the sharks than spend a day shopping, the grand Queen Victoria Building is worth a look. You can simply sit at one of the olde worlde cafés and admire the original mosaics, stained-glass windows and domed ceiling unless, of course, you're after designer fashion, contemporary art and antiques . . . **Page 59**

④ Step back in time

One of the first suburbs in Sydney to be declared a conservation area, Paddington's Victorian lacework buildings, winding tree-lined streets and rows of early 19th-century terraces offer architectural beauty, with ample opportunity to snack and sup in quaint little cafés off the main drag.
Pages 60–61

⑤ Feed the ducks

Work up an appetite in Centennial Park at the far end of Oxford St – hire a pair of rollerblades, stroll around the lakes or laze the day away under a tree.
Page 62

⑥ Art and crafty

Paddington's Saturday market is rock 'n' roll figures made out of spoons and forks, hippy baby clothes and timber photo albums mixed in with takeaway food stalls, hairbraiding and a jamboree of colourful art. Whatever you're after, it's here: brightly coloured, original and not too expensive.
Page 64

⑦ Stay out all night

Indulge in a pre-dinner cocktail, take in a Thai meal, linger over a post-dinner coffee, dance till you drop – nightlife at Kings Cross is dusk till dawn. **Pages 63, 65, 66–67**

The Australian Museum

Founded in 1827 as a natural history showcase, today it's a museum with a mission – that of helping people understand the impact humans have on the natural environment. A mixture of the fascinating and the forgettable.

A guided tour can help you make sense of the skulls and skins, skeletons and fossils, reptiles and relics. There's also an excellent indigenous section, which traces the aboriginals' lot since the settlers arrived in Australia in a clear and accessible way. Highlights include:

Level 2

Bird, spiders and reptile collection: with over 70,000 feathered specimens, you can get a close-up of the birds that flashed past in a national park before you could train your binoculars. There's also a 100-year-old crocodile, and spiders such as the dangerous funnel web or the long-legged barking spider, Australia's largest with a legspan of up to 16cm.

The museum's newest collection, **Biodiversity**, is an interactive, pick-up-and-read display to help people understand the interdependency between plants, animals and humans with plenty of examples relating what will befall the world if you leave a tap dripping or throw detergent down the sink. Some of it is over-worthy, leaving you longing to join in the child-friendly activity of dressing up as a dinosaur.

Disgusting to some, beautiful to others, an eight-month-old human foetus, donated to the museum over 100 years ago, forms part of the **human evolution** displays, alongside a recreation of the 'laetoli' tracks – the footprints preserved for over 3.6 million years in volcanic ash in Tanzania which prove that our primate ancestors did indeed walk upright.

Level 1

The life-long passion of **Albert Chapman**, this collection of over 67,000 minerals, rocks and meteorites contains specimens of all stages of **Australian mining history**.

Ground level

Eric the **opalised pliosaur**, a fast-swimming marine predator over 110 million years old, was found in Cooper Pedy in 1987. 'Eric' was delivered to the museum as a box of bones which scientists spent over 450 hours piecing together. A radio appeal to buy him in 1993 captured the imagination of Australia, raising the necessary half a million dollars.

Dinosaur-loving children will enjoy seeing the 130 million-year-old, 9m-long **Afrovenator**, which was discovered in 1993 in Africa.

The **aboriginal section** of the Australian Museum offers fascinating insights into indigenous culture, documenting the close relationship aborigines had with the land, how knowledge was passed on through the generations and the effect that white colonisation has had on aboriginal health. Particularly interesting are the personal testimonies (on video) from the 'stolen generation' – a government practice particularly popular from World War II to 1969 which separated aboriginal children from their parents and placed them with white families to learn to think and act 'white'.

Getting there: 6 College St. Tel: (02) 9320 6000. Open daily 0930–1700. Tours on the hour 1000–1500 Mon–Fri, 1100–1300 Sun. $$. Martin Place station, Bus 311/12, 441. Sydney Explorer.

Centrepoint Tower

Market St. Open Sun–Fri 0930–2130, Sat 0930–2330. $$. St James station, most buses running along Castlereagh St.

It's the tallest building in Australia at 305m, with three 12m steel statues – a gymnast, basketball player and sprinter – currently clinging to the top in celebration of the Olympics. You can take a lift to the top for a bird's-eye view or you can eat in one of the tower's revolving restaurants, self-service or *à la carte* – they're pricey but the views come free.

Hyde Park

St James/Museum station, Elizabeth St buses – 380, 382, L82.

This delightful park in the centre of Sydney was home to early sporting events in the city and a racetrack in the early

1900s. These days it's a great place for taking a moment to smell the roses (or to watch the ibis birds). Within the lush leafy grounds, there's a peaceful **Pool of Reflection** and the elegant art-deco **Anzac Memorial** to Australia's war heroes. It houses a small war museum and the eternal flame (*open daily 0900–1700; free*).

Martin Place

Martin Place station.

Martin Place adds a note of levity to this sombre area of the city, peppered with banks and business institutions. It's a great place to hang around at lunchtime as there are usually free concerts taking place in the little amphitheatre. The **cenotaph memorial** is the focus of the **Anzac Day** memorial services on 25 April.

Shops in the city centre

St James/Martin Place station, many 300 number buses (eg 301–4, 323–5).

Pitt St in the city centre is a shopping mall mecca with a cluster of centres housing large department stores, state-wide chain stores and classy one-off boutiques. Don't miss the **Queen Victoria Building (QVB)**. Built in the 1890s to replace the original Sydney markets, the QVB is an architectural gem with a domed roof and cupolas. It's currently home to over 190 individual shops built into ornate archways. They range from fancy clothes shops to quality souvenir shops, antique shops, galleries and jewellers. However, it hasn't always been a prized historical building. In 1963, the original cupolas were sold for scrap and, by the 1980s, it was earmarked for demolition. Luckily a Malaysian company stepped in and restored it. Turn-of-the-century features include a beautiful stained-glass cartwheel window and original mosaic floors. Gallery 2 contains royal 'curios' such as a hanging royal clock with moving UK monarchs, a replica of the British Crown Jewels and a tableau of the Queen Victoria's coronation in 1838.

The QVB

With a biting recession squeezing Sydney's craftsmen at the end of the 19th century, the Romanesque architecture of the QVB was deliberately elaborate in order to provide jobs for the unemployed stonemasons, plasterers and stained-glass window artists.

59

QVB: *cnr George St and Market St. Guided tours leave from information desk, daily 1130 and 1430. Tel: (02) 9264 9209. Town Hall station, many buses including 431–8.*

St Mary's Cathedral

College St. Open daily 0630–1830. St James station, buses 200, 312, 441.

St Mary's Chapel was built on the first land granted to the Roman Catholic Church in Australia in 1821. The chapel burnt down in 1865 and was replaced with the gothic-style cathedral you see today. The initial section was opened in 1882, although the two front towers in William Wardell's original design are still missing their spires. The government is currently trying to raise $5 million to rectify this. It is one of the world's largest churches, with six beautiful altars made from New Zealand stone, a replica of Michelangelo's *Pietà* and a truly stunning terrazzo mosaic floor in the crypt.

Paddington

Paddington, at the far end of Oxford St, is a mixture of the bohemian, arty and relentlessly trendy. It's the hub of the city's fashion industry and home to many local artists. This, along with its excellent Saturday market, makes it the ultimate browse-and-buy area.

Whilst Oxford St has variety, colour and character, a meander off into the side roads displays a prettier side of Paddington with some of Sydney's best examples of 1900s lacework (elaborate wrought-iron) balconies.

A walking tour of Paddington

Originally considered one of the slummiest areas of Sydney, a stroll around the beautiful back streets explains why it's now one of Sydney's most sought-after areas.

Head down **Glenmore Rd**, past some lovely lacework iron balconies to **Liverpool St**, which is well known for its long rows of Victorian terraces and more lacework. Turn right into **Spring St**, then left into **Prospect St** and **Gipps St**. These are the oldest streets in Paddington with single-storey brick houses and two-storey, four-room dwellings built in the 1840s to house the workers who were building the Victoria Barracks. A right turn into **Shadforth St** takes you past corrugated-iron-roofed buildings and offers a good view over the convict-built Victoria Barracks.

Walk along Oxford St to the **Town Hall** (1891) with arches and balustraded balconies. It now houses a theatre, cinema and library. On the other side of the road on the corner of **Ormond St** is the ornate **Post Office** (1885) and **Juniper Hall**, the oldest example of a Georgian villa in Australia. Completed in 1824, it was built by convict settler Robert Cooper, a distiller publican and self-confessed smuggler. He named the house after the berries used to distil his gin.

Then turn down Ormond St. Between 56a and 56b, there's a small fragment of a Georgian mansion, called **Engerhurst**, which was built in 1835.

Take a right turn into **Olive St**, where you can just see an early colonial home dating from 1869 above the drawings of a children's nursery. Follow the road down to the **Five Ways** roundabout, the hub of village life, with the lovely **Royal Hotel** (1888) with cast-iron balconies. Head straight over into **Gurner St**, then right into Cascade Street, which is lined by beautiful 1880s' two-storey terraces. Turn left into the lacework-decorated **Hargrave St**, then right into Elizabeth St, followed by a right turn into Underwood St, named after Thomas Underwood, a convict from the First Fleet who sold the land granted to him and headed back to Britain a richer man. Underwood St is intersected by William St – you can take a detour here to quirky shops or pop in for a beer at the attractive blue and white London Tavern (1875) on the corner of Underwood St and William St. And finally you'll come out at Paddington Inn on the corner of Oxford St.

Getting there: Museum station, then/or Bus 378, 380, 382 or L82 up Oxford St.

Paddington's terraces

Paddington's terraces were constructed by small-time builders who bought plots of land at auction, built a house for their family, then another one to let. The elaborate lacework on the façades was an exercise in one-upmanship. To give the impression of opulence, they competed with each other, adding ever more ornate designs, with ironwork lace frills beneath the balconies and extravagant tiling and plasterwork.

Centennial Park

Far end of Oxford St. Open Mar–Apr, Sept–Oct 0600–1800, May–Aug 0630–1730, Nov–Feb 0600–2000. Many buses including 378, 380, 382.

It's Sydney's biggest park and a popular picnic spot, with cycle tracks, football pitches, lily and duck ponds. Rollerblades are a great way to explore. From December to mid February, **Moonlight cinema** (open air) is held in the amphitheatre.

> **"** *I would stay [in the Cross] briefly on visits from Melbourne in the late '60s – it was a tapestry of rock and roll, flared clothes, underground publications, communal experiments and being kind to each other over sitar music and herbal tea. Sex with strangers was little more disreputable than violence on TV.* **"**
>
> **Graeme Blundell, actor, writer and director, *Places in the Heart***

Laughing Museum

16 Elizabeth St. Tel: (02) 9360 0458. Open Tue–Sat 1000–1800, Sun 1200–1600. Free.

The brainchild of **Frederic Berjot**, an eccentric and very French Frenchman, this collection of contemporary sculpture is almost wholly inspired by body art – feet stick out of the wall, hands clasp each other, backs stretch languidly. He's an unpretentious, entertaining character and the work's so reasonably priced you can afford to ship it.

Kings Cross

Kings Cross station, Bus 311, 333 or both Explorer buses.

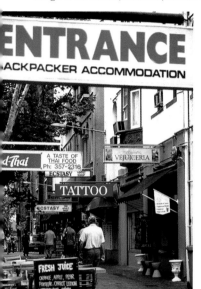

Kings Cross is an 'in yer face' area of Sydney, famed for its dusk-till-dawn nightlife, excellent restaurants and bars and seedy red-light district. At night time, neon bosoms and bottoms light up Darlinghurst Rd whilst black-suited, broad-shouldered bouncers shout out the merits of their 'adult shows'.

However, it's not all tack and brass. The area boasts some fabulous late-1800s' architecture, and just a short walk from the sleazy 'Strip' are some of the best restaurants Sydney has to offer, encompassing all manner of cuisine along Bayswater Rd and Victoria St.

63

Elizabeth Bay House

7 Onslow Ave, Elizabeth Bay. Tel: (02) 9356 3022. Open Tue–Sun 1000–1630. $. Sydney Explorer, Bus 311.

Known as the 'finest house in the colony', this magnificent Greek Revival villa was built in 1839 for the Colonial Secretary. Today, original 19th-century décor and furnishings offer a glimpse of early Australian history. A must for antique lovers, it often hosts exhibitions on interior design.

pping

Paddington market

Cnr Newcombe and Oxford St.
Saturday 1000–1600. The commercial
outlet for some of Sydney's most
innovative contemporary designers,
and an excellent place to pick up
original items.

Di Nuovo

92–94 William St. Meet Moschino
dresses, Chanel belts, Sportsgirl suits
and a variety of handbags second time
around at a fraction of the price. **Pelle**,
next door, offers the same deal on shoes.

Fashion Designer's Emporium

74 Victoria St. Creative accessories and
clothes at accessible prices – the work
of up-and-coming Australian designers
and fashion students.

Pitt St shopping malls

Centrepoint Shopping Centre:
clothing, costume jewellery and real
gems. Try the **Wilderness Society
Shop** for books on bushwalking and
native plants and animals. **Sydney
Central Plaza** has trendy boutiques
and **Grace Bros**, a large department
store. **Skygarden** stocks upmarket
fashion, homewares and a fabulous
food court. Check out **Artiques and
Country** for sake sets, Vietnamese
lacquerware and ceramics or **The
Strand** for Victorian architecture,
fancy boutiques and jewellery.
Strandbags has fancy handbags
and reasonably priced luggage, and
Strand Hatters the best bush hats.

David Jones is Sydney's premier
department store. The **MLC Centre**,
Castlereagh St contains exclusive
designer and jewellery shops: Cartier,
Gucci, Salvatore Ferragamo.

What to buy

For 'Australiana' souvenirs, head
to the QVB. Try Blue Gum Designs
for aboriginal artefacts, Best of
Australiana for souvenirs, Heaven
& Earth for paintings.

Restaurants and cafés

Paddington

Belly Dance Café

*210 Oxford St. Open Wed–Sun
0900–1800. $.* John serves up focaccia
melts, fabulous lemon meringue and
chocolate cake, whilst wife Rosalind
gives belly dancing lessons.

Beluga on Oxford

*340 Oxford St. Tel: (02) 9380 4825.
Open daily 1030–2100. $.* Pick any
freshly caught creature of the sea and
they will cook it for you, to take away
with chips or salad.

Café Brioni

*Cnr Paddington market. Tel: (02) 9360
6854. Open daily 0700–1800. $$.* It's
bursting at the seams on Saturday, but
enjoy the bands who busk near by over
an all-day breakfast or a sandwich.

The Chocolate Factory

*8 Elizabeth St. Tel: (02) 9331 3785.
Open daily until 1700. $.* This quaint
café serves up spectacular sandwiches
and biscuits with a home-cooked twist.

La Mensa

257 Oxford St. Tel: (02) 9332 2963. Open Mon–Thur 1100–2200, Fri 1100–2300, Sat 0900–2300, Sun 0900–2200. $$. Italian dishes are served at long communal metal tables. Or opt for an antipasto take-away from the adjoining deli. Top it off with a visit to the adjoining contemporary photography gallery (*open Tue–Sun, 1100–1800*).

Micky's

268 Oxford St. Tel: (02) 9361 5157. Open daily 0900–midnight. $$. The sunny garden at the back is great for a lunchtime bagel, or a robust dinner of sausages, mash and onion gravy.

Things to try

If the shopping crowds have raised your blood pressure, rollerblade back to sanity in Centennial Park. Skates are for hire on an hourly basis from **Total Skate** (*36 Oxford St; tel: (02) 9380 6356; open daily 1000–1800*).

Oxford St to Kings Cross

Darley St Thai

28–30 Bayswater Rd. Tel: (02) 9358 6530. Open daily 1830–2230. $$$. Beautifully elegant surroundings matched by the fragrant, aromatic dishes and polite, helpful waiters.

Fu-Manchu

249 Victoria St, Darlinghurst. Tel: (02) 9360 9424. Open daily 1200–1500, 1730–2230. $. Sit on the red soy-sauce-top stools for a Japanese banquet of rice noodles with roast duck.

Tropicana

227b Victoria St, Darlinghurst. Tel: (02) 9360 9809. Open 0500–midnight. $. The original formica café, famed for its huge portions, value for money and colourful clientele. Popular for early morning coffee and late-night pastas.

Una's

338–340 Victoria St, Darlinghurst. Tel: (02) 9360 6885. Open daily 0630–2300. $$. Austrian-German home-cooking at its best, with hearty portions of schnitzel, bratwurst and beef goulash.

Venice Beach

3 Kellett St. Tel: (02) 9326 9928. Open daily till late. $. A couple of minutes' walk from the Cross, decent dinners are served for a tiny fistful of dollars on the glorious candlelit garden terrace.

City centre

Hyde Park Café

Behind the Museum underground. Open Mon–Sat 0600–1600. $. Welcome the morning with strong, frothy coffee, muffins and savoury pastries.

The Strand Mall has some excellent cafés – try the olde worlde **Harris Coffee Shop**, the **Strand Expresso** for light lunches, The **Olive Italian Food Bar** for take-away sandwiches and the top-floor **Cigano** for Japanese dishes and tapas-size snacks.

Courtyard Café

Martin Place. Tel: (02) 9233 4937. Open Mon–Sat 0700–2000. $$. A good place to catch the free lunchtime concerts in Martin Place over pasta, focaccia, soup or salad.

Oxford Street

Oxford St is central to Sydney's gay scene, a colourful area of outrageously made-up transvestites and taut T-shirted muscle men. It's a focal point for the month-long gay and lesbian **Mardi Gras** *in February, which has been commemorating the Greenwich Village's Stonewall Riots since 1978.*

PADDINGTON PEARS
• FRESH JUICES
• SMOOTHIES
• FRUIT SALAD
• HOMEMADE SALADS

Hot Gossip Deli →

Fresh Squeezed Juices!

Homemade Cookies & Fruit Slices

Gourmet Goodies →

The festival culminates here in a magnificent 600,000 people parade of feather boas, sequins, glitter and glamour. Tanning beds are booked up for months before, and beauticians work overtime to fine tune favourite personas such as George Michael, Shirley Bassey and bouffant versions of Monica Lewinsky. The floats and marching groups take three hours to snake their way from Hyde Park to the Old Showground for the 'tickets like gold dust' post-parade party. Those who fail to snap up one of the 20,000 tickets party on in Oxford St clubs before staggering home with smudged mascara around midday the

following day. In recent years, the straight community have endeavoured to muscle in on the fun, and Mardi Gras organisers struggle to keep it a celebration of gay rights rather than a funky free-for-all. During the rest of the year, some Oxford St night clubs such as **DCM** (*31–33 Oxford St*) are all things to all people, with strong links in the gay community, but still attracting a partly heterosexual crowd, whilst other venues such as the **Beauchamp Hotel** (*267 Oxford St*), **Midnight Shift** (*85 Oxford St*) and the dragshow hotspot, the **Albury Hotel** (*6 Oxford St*) are exclusively gay.

> " *A vignette at Taylor Square served to symbolise the level of tolerance that now exists in society towards a group which, not long ago, was vilified. Inside the Courthouse Hotel, probably the last straight pub on Oxford Street, half-naked Mardi Gras participants in space-age silver outfits and flamboyant matching headgear drank schooners happily alongside middle-aged, working-class heterosexual couples and crusty old blokes in cardigans, who in turn seemed wholly unthreatened by their drinking partners.* "
>
> **Sydney Morning Herald**,
> **1 March 1999**

But despite the camping up, frock shocks and fun, the parade is also used to make serious political points. The 1999 Mardi Gras included a float called **Carr Attacks**, an attempt to focus the government's attention before the election on legal recognition for same-sex relationships and bringing the age of consent for gay men in line with that for heterosexuals.

Sydney beaches and Homebush Bay

If sport's your bag, Sydney's your city. The many sandy bays and beaches offer a chance to surf, dive deep into the underwater world or jog along coastal paths amidst great-to-be-alive scenery. They're a reminder that many of the city's treasures are gifts from the gods, where enjoyment is free, unstructured and in tune with the elements. At the opposite end of the spectrum, serious sport takes place at the brand-new Homebush Bay Olympic complex, where every sporting facility is finely tuned, primped and polished to the highest degree.

SYDNEY BEACHES AND HOMEBUSH BAY

BEST OF

Sydney beaches & Homebush Bay

Getting there: **Bondi:** *Train to Bondi Junction then/or bus 380, 382 or 389 from Circular Quay, Bondi & Bay Explorer. Come Sunday for the craft and second-hand market.*
Watson's Bay: *Bondi and Bay Explorer, bus 324, 325, L24, Doyle's water taxi from Harbour Master steps at Circular Quay.* **Manly:** *Ferry from Circular Quay.* **Taronga Zoo:** *Ferry from Circular Quay, bus 247.* **Homebush Bay:** *Train from Central to Olympic Park, RiverCat from Circular Quay.* **Palm Beach:** *Bus 190*

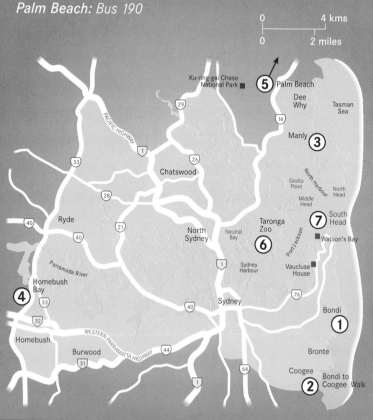

SYDNEY BEACHES AND HOMEBUSH BAY

① Beach bums

Bondi is Australia's most famous beach, and despite the hype, this long sweep of golden sand doesn't disappoint. It's boisterous, it's vibrant, it's packed full of tanned surfers, body beautifuls and every variation in between. And when you're done to a turn, there's a trendy swag of cafés and restaurants where you can chill out over a Toohey or two. **Pages 72–73**

② From Bondi to Coogee

You cannot help but be at peace with the world as you saunter along this coastal path, sea breeze in your hair, sun on your face and fabulous ocean views unfolding before you. **Page 73**

③ Nice and Manly

Worth a trip for the ferry ride alone, Manly bills itself as 'seven miles from Sydney and a thousand miles from care'. Unlike many of the city's beaches, which slot unobtrusively into the scenery like a waterside park, Manly has the merry-go-round atmosphere of a full-blown beach and holiday resort. It's a top surfing spot, and home to the fabulous Manly to Spit coastal walk. **Pages 74–75**

④ Train for the Olympics

Take a tour of Olympic Park, the Homebush Bay Olympic site: slip behind the scenes into the VIP suites and see the stadiums where the world's greatest sportsmen and women will compete. **Pages 76–77**

⑤ Hobnob with TV stars

Sydney's millionaires' playground is at Palm Beach, where fancy cars are *de rigueur* and taut-buttocked hunks and large-breasted women cavort in the surf filming the outdoor scenes for the Australian soap opera, *Home and Away*. Leave the glitz and head for wonderful walks and its wild national park, just a ferry ride away. **Page 78**

⑥ Talk with the animals

Taronga Zoo is no ordinary zoo – it's a cliff-top zoo winding down into Mosman Bay. Not only can you see the Tasmanian Devil, kangaroos and Australia's fascinating egg-laying mammal, the elusive duckbilled platypus, you can also enjoy a bird's-eye view over Sydney. **Page 79**

⑦ Languish over lobster

Doyles Fish Restaurant is one of Sydney's oldest institutions and the panoramic journey there by water taxi from Circular Quay just serves to whet your appetite. Once you've indulged in a fresh seafood feast, you can work it off with a walk to the craggy headland of South Head. **Pages 80–81**

Tourist information

Manly Visitors Information Bureau: *Ocean Beach, North Steyne, Manly. Tel: (02) 9977 1088. Open daily 1000–1600.*
Homebush Bay Visitors Centre: *Homebush Bay. Tel: (02) 9735 4800. Open daily 0900–1700. Website: www.oca.nsw.gov.au*

Bondi and around

This big sweep of golden sand has been the focus of Australian beach culture for over 100 years. Whatever bad publicity Bondi might have received for its car thefts, drugs culture and loutish tourists drinking in the sun, it's still a stunning sight.

Once the domain of the working classes, today Bondi is cosmopolitan with a sprinkling of upmarket restaurants and trendy shops. Frequented by locals, backpackers and home to a large immigrant community, it's a tableau of outdoor living with tanned torsos heading surfwards and micro bikinis flouting the safe tanning rules. Topless bathing is tolerated around South Bondi – a change from the 1960s when beach inspectors measured women's bikinis to check that their bottom halves conformed to the four-inch-fabric rule.

Tamarama beach: a 20-minute walk from Bondi, this attractive sandy cove is nicknamed 'Glamarama' because of its popularity with beautiful people, particularly handsome men and body-conscious gays. When the wind's blowing in the right direction, it's a top surfing spot.

Bronte Beach is nicknamed 'the thinking man's Bondi' because it tends to attract creative types – actors, writers and several celebrities. It's also a popular family spot with a convenient swag of cafés just over the road. *Bus 378 from Oxford St.*

Clovelly Beach: the least beautiful of the five beaches, it's good for novice swimmers as it's more like a creek. It's an excellent area for snorkelling (look out for giant groper) and those who live in fear of being coshed on the head by a surfboard can relax – they're banned for most of the day. *Bus 339 from Circular Quay.*

Coogee is a few kilometres south of Bondi, but similar in atmosphere (with less ferocious surf) and less crowded. This beach is a backpackers' hang-out and, consequently, pretty lively in the evenings, although the entertainment tends to be busy pubs selling schooners of beer at knock-down prices. *Buses 373, 374 from Circular Quay, train to Bondi Junction then 314 or 315.*

From Bondi to Bronte and Coogee

The coastal walk from Bondi to **Clovelly** is spectacular. Populated with power-walkers, joggers, dog walkers and people just watching the sea, it's a real celebration of outdoor life. Join the path at the southern end of Bondi, which leads along the coast to **Tamarama** and **Bronte**. After Bronte, take the coastal road through the sandstone cliffs, a favourite spot for climbers trying out their techniques. Continue through **Waverley Cemetery**, with huge family vaults and graves dating back to the mid 1800s. It sounds morbid but perched on the cliff tops with the preponderance of wild flowers, the sea breeze and wonderful views, it's hard to imagine a more idyllic place for eternal rest. This will lead you to Clovelly and on to **Gordon's Bay**, which has a 620m underwater nature trail marked by chains and drums for divers. After Gordon's Bay the walk is mostly through suburban streets to the long sweep of pale sand at **Coogee**, where you can enjoy a swim in **Wiley's Baths**, an Olympic-size pool cut into the rocks. There's also a women-and-children-only pool, where the secluded location between cliffs and bush means that females can shed their bikini tops without being leered at.

73

" *1999, after years of furious gentrification, saw Bronte officially elevated to café apotheosis with the visit of the king of self-employed businessmen, Rupert Murdoch. With his new lady-friend on one arm, and chaperoned by Lachlan and Sarah, Mr Murdoch arranged himself rather uncomfortably at an outside table at Sejuiced and shared two smoothies with his family. The waitress with fire-engine red hair couldn't have cared less. The rest of us were rubbernecking like geese on ecstasy.* "

Katherine Biber, Sydney Sidewalk web page

Manly

Just over 11km ('seven miles' as it's billed) from Sydney, Manly is the most accessible of the northern beaches, with a lively holiday atmosphere. The Corso, which leads from the wharf to the long stretch of sand, is a commercialised, anywhere-in-the-world, seaside-resort high street.

However, away from the take-away cartons, sunburnt shoulders and back-to-front baseball caps, Manly has real charm. It's worth making the trip for the front-seat panoramic view from the ferry alone.

Heritage and history

Look beyond the fish and chips, and you will see some wonderful architecture in Manly. It ranges from the art-nouveau circular windows and garland decorations above shops on the Corso to the microcosm of styles in Ashburner St, which encompass Victorian Italianate cottages with cast-iron columns (Nos 18 and 20) and art-deco architecture such as the waterfall motifs (Adastra, No 8). The excellent *Heart of Manly Heritage Walk* publication (Manly Tourist Information) is an informative historical walk around Manly's hidden treasures.

Manly to Spit Bridge – Manly Scenic Walkway

This beautiful 10km coastal walk is among the best in Sydney. It takes in panoramic views of Sydney Harbour, aboriginal shell middens and suburban city life, pockets of rainforest, native bushland and a myriad of wildflowers and colourful birds. It's a mixture of easy walking and rough, steep slopes with plenty of secluded beaches and bays to refresh yourself along the way. Pick up the *Manly Scenic Walkway Guide* from the tourist office for an explanation of points of interest along the way.

Manly beach

Infamous for its fabulous surf, Manly was the first beach in Sydney to allow surfing and daylight swimming in 1903. Nearly three-quarters of a century later, liberalism triumphed again when the first legal topless and nude beach was established at **Reef Beach**, on the way to the Spit. Today a host of **surf competitions** and **lifesaving carnivals** (January) takes place at Manly beach, along with **volleyball championships** (January), and the **Ironman and Ironwomen championships** (February).

Oceanworld

West Esplanade, Manly Wharf. Tel: (02) 9949 2644. Open daily 1000–1730. $$.

Admire the wonders of the world beneath the sea from giant underwater walkways with sharks, stingrays, giant turtles and beautiful corals from the Great Barrier Reef. If you haven't been to Sydney's Aquarium, pop in here. You can also swim with the sharks or the Australian and New Zealand fur seals. Advance booking essential for shark/fur seal swims.

Shelly beach

A 20-minute walk east along Marine Parade, this smaller beach offers great diving and a friendly family atmosphere. It's a lovely walk, dotted with ocean-inspired sculptures by local artists, one of the many public art projects throughout NSW.

Take to your wheels

The beachside Marine Parade (*North Steyne*), lined with its famous Norfolk pines, is the perfect (flat!) ground to take your first rollerblade steps. If you're already an experienced rollerblader, **Keirle Park** in North Manly has jumps, mini ramps and a horseshoe bowl. Rollerblades and lessons are available from **Manly Blades** (*Shop 2, 49 North Steyne; tel: (02) 9976 3833*).

Olympic Park

Previously a brickworks, armaments depot, abattoir and then industrial dumping ground, the impressive sports complex at Homebush Bay has been transformed into the main site for the Olympic Games in 2000. For the first time ever, all the athletes and officials will be housed in the same village. The majority of Olympic events will take place in Homebush Bay's state-of-the-art facilities, which include an archery park and tennis centre, plus an athletics centre, stadium and aquatic centre. Important sporting venues include:

The Aquatic Centre (*open to the public daily 0500–2200; $*): This is the only facility in the world to have the warm-up (training) pool and competition pool under the same roof. As well as a capacity to increase seating from 4400 to 15,000, there are lots of snazzy features in the Aquatic Centre – the training pool has a fibreglass floor, which can be moved up and down, even doubling up as a fashion catwalk on occasion. The 5m-deep diving pool has bubbles rippling the surface, so divers from the 10m tower can see where to aim for. And for novice divers, a big 'bubble surge' cushions their experimental splats. There's also a huge leisure area with castles, spurting volcanoes and a rapid river ride.

> " *Bob Carr power-walks and swims. But you would never call him a sporting type . . . How ironic that this most intellectual of premiers is presiding over the greatest expenditure on organised sport in modern history . . . The irony is NSW citizens are a bit like Carr. They jog and swim but they are not sports-crazy like Melburnians. Who is going to use these facilities once the Olympic family packs its designer bags and departs?* "

Adele Horin, *Sydney Morning Herald***, 27 February 1999**

The International Athletics Centre will be used for training and warm-ups during the games, with a capacity of 15,000 people, whilst the privately owned **Athletics Stadium**, with seating for 110,000 spectators, will be used for track and field events, the closing stages of the Marathon and the Gold Medal soccer final during the Olympics. Thereafter, it will double up as a sporting

and concert venue. It has a special roof that shades the spectators and minimises shadows on the playing area.

Sydney is hosting the 'greenest' Olympic games in history. Solar panels fuel lighting, heating and gas-assisted hot water tanks, ventilation is wind-powered. Air-conditioning in the Aquatic Centre is limited to the area around spectator seats, so that the atmosphere doesn't cool the pool temperature. But best of all, the Aquatic Centre makes such good use of natural light that only ten artificial ones are needed.

Take a tour

The informative Behind the Scenes tour of the International Aquatic Centre and Athletics Centre takes in both buildings, a stroll through the leisure area and a look around the VIP rooms, followed by a swim in the leisure pools (*Mon–Fri 1000, 1200, 1400; weekends 1200, 1400. Bookings, tel: (02) 9752 3666. $$*).

Getting there: Homebush Bay. Train from Central to Olympic Park. RiverCat ferry from Circular Quay to Homebush Bay.

Palm Beach

The most northern of the Sydney beaches, this wonderfully terracotta stretch of sand is the filming backdrop for the Australian soap, *Home and Away*. Well known as a playground for the rich and famous, it's a big holiday home area, with wealthy families building million-dollar houses which they occupy for just a couple of weeks a year. The **Pittwater** inlet to the west is a great spot for cruising, boating and fishing.

Barrenjoey headland

Park near the lighthouse, for a daily fee, double at weekends.

This picturesque peninsula is edged by the beautiful Palm Beach on the east and the rather grey, weedy Station Beach to the west. A convict-built walking trail lined with bottlebrushes and wildflowers takes you over the sandstones and up to the lighthouse, affording fabulous views over both sides of the headland. It's a peaceful place to picnic – a short track in front of the lighthouse will take you to a rocky plateau opposite **Lion Island**. For a different return route, follow **Smuggler's Trail**, a rough track down between the two cottages. It peters out in places so be prepared for a bit of climbing and scrambling.

Getting there: L90/190 bus from Wynyard, York St. By car: take Route 14, signposted to Mosman and Manly, after the Harbour Bridge. Follow it to Spit Bridge, continue north along the coast past Dee Why and Collaroy. Take Barrenjoey Rd at Mona Vale. Fly by seaplane from Sydney's Rose Bay with Sydney Harbour Seaplanes (tel: 1800 803 558) or South Pacific Seaplanes (tel: (02) 9544 0077).

No to *Baywatch*

Avalon beach, another glorious stretch of sand just a few kilometres south of Palm Beach, was top choice for American TV series Baywatch*. Despite support from NSW Premier Bob Carr, locals protested that it would cause traffic congestion and infringe on their freedom to use the beach and sent all those bronzed bods to film elsewhere.*

Ku-ring-gai Chase National Park

Mona Vale Beach, Pittwater Rd (7km north of Pymble). Gates are locked at 1800 winter, 2030 summer. $$ per day. There's a small charge for day-trippers landing by ferry or boat.

Just 26km north of Sydney, this is a wild and unspoilt park. Highlights include the **West Head**, which offers a fabulous view over Broken Bay, Lion Island and 'the world's largest ocean highway', the commuter belt for dolphins, whales and seals.

The Basin is a 2.8km walk through scrubland and forest, that passes an aboriginal rock engravings site. The downhill walk, which is very steep in places, leads to a peaceful, tree-shaded bay with a camping area, pretty beach and a view across to the Barrenjoey lighthouse. Picnic amongst the kookaburras and wallabies.

The Palm Beach Ferry Service (*tel: (02) 9918 7247*) runs from Palm Beach wharf to the Basin hourly. **By car:** From Sydney, take the Pacific Highway, then take the Mona Vale Road through St Ives, turning off at Terrey Hills for the McCarrs Creek Rd entrance.

Taronga Zoo

Bradleys Head Rd, Mosman. Open daily 0900–1700. $$.

This zoo enjoys a splendid location on the cliffs overlooking Sydney harbour. It's home to over 3000 animals and well worth a visit if you don't have time to make excursions to see native animals in their natural habitat. During the day there are various keeper talks on animals such as chimpanzees, gorillas, dingoes and penguins, plus feeding times, free-flight bird shows, seal shows and koala encounters.

Getting there: Ferry to Taronga Zoo, bus 247. Aerial safari ride (cable car) to the top if you don't fancy the walk. A Zoo Pass ticket (available at Circular Quay ferry) will save you money – it includes return ferry and bus trips, Zoo admission and the aerial safari ride.

Watson's Bay

Ferry to Watson's Bay, Doyles water taxi from Circular Quay (weekday lunchtimes only), bus L24, 324, 325, Bondi & Bay Explorer.

Try it yourself

For fish fans who want to replicate the delicious sea trout, whiting and snapper dishes back home, look out for the fabulous Alice Doyle's Fish Cookbook, *which is the last word in tasty seafood. Available in bookstores and at Doyles Fish Restaurant.*

Watson's Bay is famous for its long-established fish restaurant, **Doyles**. There are three variations of this famous eaterie situated in a picturesque bay. The original restaurant, Doyles on the Beach, is reminiscent of a large green and white beach hut and was founded in 1885. It attracts a mixed crowd for its mouth-watering seafood dishes ranging from Tweed Heads Pearl Perch fillets to the acclaimed Sydney Rock Oysters and straightforward fish and chips. Doyles on the Wharf offers a similar menu. For speed and economy, there's an adjoining take-away fish and chip shop. The views back over Sydney are wonderful.

The Gap

On the ocean side of the headland, opposite Watson's Bay, is a panoramic coastal walk that takes in **Gap Park**, once an important military position for guarding the harbour. Now the area is better known for the Gap, a large fissure in the cliffs which is a popular suicide spot. Further along the cliff path is the anchor belonging to the *Dunbar*, which was shipwrecked 457m south of the Gap in 1857 when the Captain mistook the harbour entrance. One hundred and twenty-one people died, with a sole survivor found clinging to rocks near by.

Vaucluse House

Wentworth Rd, Vaucluse. Tel: (02) 9388 7922. Open Tue–Sun 1000–1630.
Bondi and Bay Explorer, bus 325 from Circular Quay or get off bus 324 to
Watson's Bay at the beautiful Rose Bay convent (great view over the harbour)
and walk for 20 minutes. $.

This fine 19th-century mansion set in Sydney's most exclusive suburb was the home of William Wentworth, a

famous explorer, author and politician in early colonial days. He lived there with his wife, Sarah, and their ten children from 1827 to 1862. The building started life as a small cottage, to which Wentworth added many rooms including lavish entertaining rooms and children's and servants' bedrooms. The house contains some original 19th-century furniture and décor and is set in lovely gardens. Wentworth's gothic-style mausoleum is a couple of streets away on the right, down Chapel Road.

Watson's Bay to South Head

From Watson's Bay, a beautiful walk north along the coast takes you through Sydney Harbour National Park to South Head, one of two headlands forming the entrance to Sydney Harbour. Take the steps at the northern end of Watson's Bay beach to Cove St, then turn right into Victoria St and left into Cliff St. This will bring you to the trendy Camp Cove beach, where a coastal track leads across the cliff tops to the pretty Lady Bay, a predominantly male nudist beach nestling in a secluded cove. From there, you can join the South Head heritage trail, which brings you to the tip of the peninsula for a fabulous view over the Tasman Sea.

Eating out

Bondi

Bondi Tratt

34 Campbell Parade, Bondi. Tel: (02) 9365 4303. Open daily for breakfast, lunch and dinner. Licensed and BYO. $$. Always busy, this is a favourite with the locals, so you need to book. Delicious dishes range from roasted tomato risotto with parmesan and rocket to pork and pistachio nut sausages, with a choice of lively indoor atmosphere or a backdrop of the starry night sky.

Hugos

70 Campbell Parade, Bondi. Tel: (02) 9300 0900. Open daily 1800–2300 plus brunch and lunch at weekends, 0900–1600. $$$. The people are smart and slender, the service swish, the cuisine modern Australian with a strong Pacific influence. Succulent fish and meat dishes are cooked to perfection with soy, ginger and spices and served up with a stunning view over Bondi.

Star Fish Bar Café

178 Campbell Parade. Tel: (02) 9300 0622. Open daily, lunch and dinner. $$. Part of the pink Hotel Bondi, the large shady terrace buzzes to the sound of a young crowd drinking designer beers and eating their way through Mediterranean-influenced dishes such as pumpkin and spinach lasagne and clam chowder.

Bronte

Jenny's Café

Open daily 0630–1700 (winter), later in summer. $. Enjoy a beach view over a breakfast of banana bread, toast with homemade jam or fruit salad. It's a friendly place to hang out and the food, like the décor, is fresh and clean.

Sejuiced

Open daily 0630–1700, later in summer and at weekends. $. Head here for a refreshing or disgustingly (literally) healthy juice. It also does some excellent salads and plates piled high with pasta.

Manly

La Galerie

The Corso. $. This large food court has a communal seating area servicing a range of take-away restaurants including Indian, seafood, sushi and health food.

Greens Eatery

1–3 Sydney Rd, just off the Corso. Open daily 0800–1800. $. A super-healthy, super-wholesome lentil, rissole and rice café. Eat in or take-away, there's a little terrace outside for newspaper perusing and even after a generous portion of lebanese pitta followed by a slab of cake, you'll still get change from a blue note.

Le Kiosk

Shelly Beach. Tel: (02) 9977 4122. Open daily lunch and dinner. $$$. Just metres from the beach, with a terrace under the palm trees, this is fine dining at its best. The menu is sprinkled with fancy ingredients, confits and parfaits, and desserts to die for.

Palm Beach and around

La Palma

1108 Barrenjoey Rd. Tel: (02) 9974 4001. Open daily lunch and dinner. $$$. Authentic Northern Italian cuisine served in blissful surroundings, against a backdrop of jazz music, sea views and ocean breeze.

On the Boardwalk

24–26 Ocean Rd, Palm Beach. Tel: (02) 9974 5644. $$. Enjoy the delights of loin of kangaroo, honey, chilli and ginger prawns or snow pea and roast pumpkin fettucine. There's an upstairs balcony with sea view through the palm trees. The café downstairs serves burgers, focaccias, pasta and fish and chips.

Watsons Bay

See page 80 for descriptions of:

Doyles on the Beach

Tel: (02) 9337 2007. Open daily lunch and dinner. $$$.

Doyles on the Wharf

Tel: (02) 9337 1572. Open Wed–Sat, lunch and dinner, Mon and Tue evenings in Jan. $$$.

Messing about on the river

Visit Ku-ring-gai Chase National Park under your own steam – boats for up to six people can be hired from Gonsalves Boatshed *(* next to the ferry wharf at Palm Beach; tel: (02) 9974 4409; $$ *). Fishing tackle is also for sale. Scenic cruises around Broken Bay and the Hawkesbury River to Patonga and Bobbin Head in the national park are run by* Palm Beach Ferry Service *(* tel: (02) 9918 2747; $$ *).*

Surfing in the sun

It's a stereotype but a true one. New South Wales beaches really are packed with lads and lasses, bodies browned by the sun, striding across the sand with a surfboard under their arm. But not just anyone can join in . . . each beach has its clique. Here's the language you need to infiltrate the surfing set:

The gear

Webs: gloves where the fingers are webbed together for maximum paddling power
Boardies: (surf) board shorts
Sunnies: sunglasses
Legropes: to tie your surfboard to your ankle
Wettie: a wetsuit to stop you chilling up on colder days
Neoprene booties: tight-fitting shoes made of wetsuit material

The boards

Stick: surfboard
Gun: a very long surfboard used for riding huge breakers
Boogie board: a very short, fat surfboard

The people

Wax head/surfie: a surfer
Grommet: young version of a wax head
Speed hump/shark biscuit: a boogie/body boarder

As surfers are none too keen to share their waves with strangers, the Bondi crowd is currently up in arms about plans to build Bondi Park station at the south end of the beach. Not only are they unwilling to throw open their water to any more surfies, they also claim that the rips by the planned station site are particularly bad, so it will mean increased danger for unsuspecting visitors hopping off the train and straight into the sea. But it's not just the surfers who oppose the move. The local inhabitants don't want to make access to their little patch of paradise any easier than it is already, and there's also a strong suspicion that once Bondi Park station opens, it will pave the way for high-rise development in an area which, to date, has remained relatively low level. A third voice of opposition comes from the police, who feel that the drugs problem in Bondi will increase, with junkies and dealers heading beachwards with easier transport links from Kings Cross. According to the council, the train station is currently on hold until the Minister of Transport carries out an 'environmental impact assessment'. Watch this space.

BLUE MOUNTAINS AND HUNTER VALLEY

Blue Mountains and Hunter Valley

Head west to the Blue Mountains for a wander around the edge of a sandstone gorge, along paths lined with wildflowers and criss-crossed by bright crimson rosella birds ducking and diving over the hazy blue valley below. Or meander north up to the lush green vineyards of the Hunter Valley for a lazy day spent tasting rich red wines and crisp dry whites over a gourmet lunch.

Blue Mountains and Hunter Valley

*Getting there: **Blue Mountains:** head west out of Sydney from George St onto Broadway, Parramatta Rd (Great Western Highway) onto the M4 motorway. **Hunter Valley:** from Sydney, head north following Metroad 1 signs onto the Pacific Highway. Turn off onto the F1 Freeway to Newcastle exiting at Cessnock and follow signs for the vineyards. To reach Upper Hunter from Lower Hunter, take Branxton Rd to New England Highway towards Singleton, then turn off to Denman.*

① Take a walk on the wild side

Even if you 'don't do walking', the only way to get a true feel for the vast wilderness of the Blue Mountains is on foot. Head to Echo Point or Govetts Leap (Blackheath) to choose from 20-minute strolls to several hour-long hikes. Top choices: the Prince Henry Cliff walk and Pulpit Rock.
Pages 90–91

② Scare yourself silly

Abseil down a rocky gorge, or take the challenge one step further and combine it with canyoning. **Page 91**

③ Sniff and swirl

Family-run, city slick, spit and sawdust . . . Hunter Valley's vineyards are as varied as the wines themselves, so sip your shiraz, swirl the chardonnay and find out for yourself why NSW wines account for 21 per cent of Australia's exported wine. For an entertaining tour, head to Tyrell's, for informative and generous wine tasting, choose Rosemount. **Pages 92–93**

④ Go for the burn

Walk up to the summit of the self-igniting coal seams of Burning Mountain, steeped in aboriginal legend, in the company of groups of kangaroos and wedge-tailed eagles.
Page 95

⑤ Watch the world go by

Relax in the olde worlde mountain village of Leura – snap up some non-essential, yet must-have souvenirs in the arty shops dotting The Mall, chill out over a coffee, linger over a wholesome lunch. **Pages 96–97**

Organised tours:

There are many orgainised day-trips from Sydney to the Blue Mountains and Hunter Valley – try **ATS** (*tel: (02) 9555 2700*); **AAT Kinga** (*tel: (02) 9252 2788*); **Murrays** (*tel: 13 22 51*). Regualr trains operate from Sydney Central station to Leura, Katoomba (2-hour journey) and Blackheath. **Mountainlink** (*tel: (02) 4782 3333*) operates a regular shuttle bus between Katoomba station, Echo Point and Leura and Blackheath. A **Blue Mountains Explorer** bus (*tel: (02) 4782 4807*) departs from Katoomba station allowing unlimited hop-on, hop-off stops around the main Leura, Echo Point and Katoomba attractions at week-ends and public and school holidays.

Tourist information

Visitor information: *Echo Point, Three Sisters, Katoomba. Tel: (02) 4739 6266. Open daily 0900–1700. www.bluemts.com.au*
Blue Mountains Heritage Centre: *Govetts Leap Rd, Blackheath. Tel: (02) 4787 8877. Open daily 0900–1630.* Runs an excellent programme of guided walks.
Hunter Valley Wine Country Information Centre: *Turner Park, Aberdare Rd, Cessnock (approx 1km before Cessnock). Tel: (02) 4990 4477. Open Mon–Fri 0900–1700, Sat 0930–1700, Sun 0930–1530. www.winecountry.com.au*

Blue Mountains

After the bustle of cosmopolitan Sydney, the Blue Mountains, just a 100km drive west, provide a wilderness atmosphere and fresh air by the lungful. So named for the blue-tinged haze shimmering in the valleys as the sun reflects off oil droplets from the eucalyptus trees, the mountains proved to be an impenetrable barrier to the fertile western plains during early colonial days.

However, 19th-century explorers, Wentworth (*see page 81*), Blaxland and Lawson discovered a route through to the valuable grazing pastures in 1813. Present-day explorers can enjoy a mixture of stunning cliffs and gorges, wildlife and waterfalls and arty-crafty villages, dotted about on a series of plateaux divided by deep valleys.

Very coffee-and-cake-shop in atmosphere, **Leura** is a quaint village housing some upmarket galleries, restaurants and souvenir shops. It's home to the annual **Garden festival**, when private gardens are opened to the public on the second weekend in October. Just south of the centre is **Leuralla** (*36 Olympian Parade, Leura; tel: (02) 4784 1169; open daily 1000–1700; $*), a grand family home with elegant 1920s' furnishings, a toy museum and a wonderful collection of 1920–50s' clockwork, electric and steam model trains and figures. Over the road, the amphitheatre in the turn-of-the-century gardens is the perfect panoramic picnic spot. A few kilometres east of Leura is **Sublime Point**, where a steep walk to the look-out offers a fabulous view over the dense valley below.

A panoramic cliff drive from Leura weaves its way to **Echo Point**, home to the Blue Mountains' most famous rock formation, the **Three Sisters**, a cluster of 240-million-year-old sandstone outcrops. There is a short walk up to the first of the three sisters, or a strenuous, knee-knackering 896-step walk to the valley floor via the Giant Stairway.

From here, an hour's walk through giant ferns and forest brings you to the **Scenic Railway** at Katoomba (*see below*) for a lift back up. Various bushwalks start from Echo Point, including the scenic **Prince Henry Cliff** walk along the escarpment edge in either direction – east to the Leura cascades or west to Katoomba Falls.

Katoomba

Katoomba is one of the largest Blue Mountain towns. The street of most interest to tourists is Katoomba St, a mixture of second-hand shops, art-deco cafés and activity gear shops. Reservations can be made in Katoomba for abseiling, guided mountain walks, horse-riding excursions, 4WD hire for off-the-beaten-track exploring and canyoning (abseiling through waterfalls, swimming, wading through pools and scrambling over rocks). Good tour operators are **Fantastic Aussie Tours** (*283 Main St; tel: (02) 4782 1866, or 1300 300 915 outside Blue Mountains area*), and **Blue Mountains Adventure Company** (*84a Main St; tel: (02) 4782 1271, www.bmac.com.au*). **Cox's River Escapes** run environmentally friendly expeditions in small groups (*tel: (02) 4784 1621, www.bluemts.com.au/Cox's River*). *All activities: $$$, except guided walks: $$.*

For a quick thrill, the nearby **Scenic Skyway**, a panoramic cable-car ride across the Jamison Valley, is fairly heartstopping or you can plunge into the valley on the **Scenic Railway**, the world's steepest incline railway with a vertical descent of 229m (*both just south of Katoomba town centre, off Cliff Dr; open 0900–1650; $*).

A further 10km west takes you to **Blackheath**, the starting-point for some of the most spectacular bushwalks in the area, taking in waterfalls, wildflowers and a myriad of bird life. Two walks of average difficulty with rewarding views include Govetts Leap Look Out (near the visitor's centre) to Pulpit Rock, or Evans Look Out, both about a 3-hour return hike.

> " *Living in the Blue Mountains, you don't have to be reminded of starry nights. You don't have to look up on the calendar to see if there's a full moon. When there's a storm over Sydney, you don't have to watch it on the news. You don't have to go to an Oxygen Bar to breathe exquisite air. You're close to primal forces . . . it's a turbulent place to live. Elemental.* "

Richard Neville, writer and commentator,
Places in the Heart

Hunter Valley

*Centred around the village of **Pokolbin**, the lush Hunter Valley is home to over 60 wineries. The hot dust flies up from the unsealed roads that stretch endlessly through the fertile vineyards and horse paddocks against the backdrop of the Brokenback mountain range.*

On a quiet weekday, when the countryside swelters under the scorching sun, it feels as if you've strayed onto the set of *Thelma and Louise*. Wineries range from slick, internationally acclaimed outfits, to small family businesses brewing a few bottles in their back yard. In almost all of them, you can turn up for a free cellar-door tasting without obligation.

Broke Rd is home to some interesting wineries. **Peterson's Champagne House** (*tel: (02) 4998 7881; open daily 0900–1700*), on the corner, specialises in sparkling wines. **McGuigan's** (*tel: (02) 4998 7402; open daily 1000–1650; tours daily 1200*), a little further along, is a slick, professional outfit offering a whole range of wines from inexpensive Black Label chardonnays to the prestigious Personal Reserve Tawny Port. The complex encompasses several restaurants, an excellent souvenir shop and the Hunter Valley Cheese Co, where you can buy a selection of cheeses (try Mt Buffalo Blue goat's cheese) or a plate of antipasto, uncork a bottle of fine wine and enjoy the ultimate picnic at the picnic tables outside. Next door is the picturesque **Peppers Creek Winery**

> **"** We came to as fine a land as imagination can form . . . fine land fit for cultivation and equally so for grazing. **"**
>
> **John Howe, Chief Constable of Hawkesbury, exploring the Hunter Valley in 1820**

(*tel: (02) 4998 7532; open Wed–Sun 1000–1700*), where you can sample traditional handmade wines and enjoy a delicious bruschetta snack on the rose-filled terrace at the adjoining Café Enzo. You can also pop next door to the antique shop. Should love be in the air, there's a fine selection of engagement and wedding rings. Further on still is one of the oldest vineyards in Hunter, still owned by the original founding family, **Tyrell's** (*tel: (02) 4993 7000; open 0800–1700 Mon–Sat*). It offers a wonderfully entertaining vineyard tour (*1330 Mon–Sat*), run by Murray, a charming immigrant Scot, who recounts its history with panache and guides you through the wine-making process. It culminates in a plentiful wine tasting – try the inexpensive, wonderfully rich Long Flat Red – buy a case to keep in the boot for BYO emergencies.

At the far end of Gillards Rd (off Macdonalds Rd) is **Constable and Hershon** (*tel: (02) 4998 7887; open daily 1000–1700; free garden tours Mon–Fri 1030*). This unusual, boutique vineyard is the vision of two London-based Australian stockbrokers. Immaculate gardens border the vines, comprising a rose garden complete with pergola and bandstand, a herb garden, croquet lawn and a contemporary sculpture garden. Hershon's son-in-law runs the wholesale side, whilst Constable jets in regularly to titivate his gardens and add sculptures.

93

But the Hunter isn't only about sniffing and swirling. Leave the car and cycle or walk the wine trail with **Grapemobile bicycle and walking tours** (*tel: (02) 4991 2339; $$$*) or take a tour in a horse and carriage with **Pokolbin Horse Coaches** (*tel: (02) 4998 7305*) or **Paxton Brown Carriages** (*tel: (02) 4998 7362; $$–$$$*). Enjoy a dawn balloon ride over the valley through **Balloon Aloft** (*tel: 1800 028 568; $$$*) or **Hunter Valley Hot-Air Ballooning** (*tel: 1800 81 81 91; $$$*) or get in the swing at **Portofino Golf Course** (*cnr Allandale and Lovedale Rds, tel: (02) 4991 4777; $$*).

Upper Hunter Valley

There are fewer than ten wineries in Upper Hunter, spread out in a wide circle from Denman. Scenically, the area is stunning, with wineries and world-famous horse stud farms nestling amidst rolling pastures against a backdrop of scrub-covered mountains and sandstone cliffs. In recent years, the Upper Hunter Valley has been recognised as a prime grape-growing

region, with better viticulture soils, higher elevation and more reliable water supplies than the lower valley. It's home to one large wine-maker and several boutique vineyards. Visit Upper Hunter at the weekends, as many cafés and tours operate at weekends only.

The largest producer on the block is the **Rosemount Estate** (*Rosemount Rd, Denman; tel: (02) 6547 2467; open Mon–Sat 1000–1600, Sun 1030–1600*). Velvety red-roses flank the drive, and ducks lead the way to the tasting area of some of the region's most prestigious wines. There are no tours, but the wine tasting is generous with welcoming, knowledgeable staff. An attractive drive north leads to **Cruickshank Callatoota** (*Wybong Rd, Wybong; tel: (02) 6547 8149; open daily 0900–1700*), a spit-and-sawdust

Small is beautiful

Try Rosemount's premium red wines – GSM or Traditional – as the smaller quantities produced mean that the wines are largely for the domestic market. Nectar!

vineyard specialising in red wines (Cabernet Sauvignon and Cabernet Franc) plus an excellent rosé. A further 8km leads to **Reynolds Yarraman** (*Yarraman Rd, Wybong; tel: (02) 6547 8127; open Mon–Sat 1000–1600, Sun 1100–1600*), a picturesque convict-hewn sandstone building dating from 1837. Try the award-winning Semillon wines and a selection grown in the cooler climate Orange district.

Beyond Upper Hunter Valley

From Upper Hunter Valley, a worthwhile detour is to **Burning Mountain**, 20km north of Scone, after Wingen, on the New England Highway, where a naturally ignited coal seam has been smouldering on the mountainside for over 5000 years. A 35-minute walk takes you through a eucalyptus forest populated by wedge-tailed eagles to the summit, where spiralling smoke (rather than raging flames) creates an eerie atmosphere. Groups of kangaroos criss-cross your path, and can often be seen warming their paws on the summit.

A scenic route back to the coast is through the rugged wilderness of **Barrington Tops Park** (52km east of Scone). Moonan Flat to Gloucester is about a 2-hour drive on unsealed roads which, if it hasn't been raining, are just about bearable in a 2WD, though a 4WD is infinitely preferable. The rainforests, waterfalls, rivers and diverse wildlife – brush turkeys, pademelons, wallabies and wombats – make for a beautiful journey. A bad-weather alternative is to join the Oxley Highway north of Tamworth, which leads over a plateau fringed with fertile grazing pastures, winding down through pockets of rainforest to Port Macquarie.

Legendary tears

Legend has it that Burning Mountain was ignited when the wife of an aboriginal warrior cried tears of fire, on hearing of her husband's death in a battle on the Wollemi River.

Eating out

The Mall in **Leura** is home to some excellent restaurants and cafés. Try **Café Bon Ton** (*192 The Mall; tel: (02) 4782 4377; open daily breakfast, lunch and dinner; closed Tue evening; $$*), where modern Australian dishes are served in the lovely shady garden or light airy indoor café. BYO. **Loaves and The Dishes** (*180a The Mall; tel: (02) 4784 3600; $*) deals in wholesome fare: pumpkin and parmesan risotto, potato, leek and sorrel soup, Mediterranean salads but the huge chunks of chocolate/date/orange cake and fruit muffins are reason enough to come here. **Silk's Brasserie** (*128 The Mall; tel: (02) 4784 2534; open daily lunch and dinner; $$$*) is smart, yet traditional, offering hearty portions of modern Australian 'mountain' food in relaxing surroundings.

Katoomba has a preponderance of reasonably priced art-deco cafés on the street of the same name. The bright, airy **Savoy** (*26–28 Katoomba St; open daily breakfast–dinner*) has a good range of salads, focaccias and pastas, as does the friendly **Café Zuppa** (*36 Katoomba St*). **The Blues café** over the road at number 57 is a veggie and vegan haven with polenta pie, tofu burgers and wondrous desserts.

The **Hunter Valley**'s best cafés and restaurants are usually attached to wineries. **The Cellar**, part of McGuigan's (*Broke Rd; tel: (02) 4998 7584; open daily lunch and dinner, closed Sun evening; $$$*) is slick, yet welcoming, with dishes ranging from peppered lambs brains to BBQ duckling and smoked kangaroo served in a candlelit garden room, with log fires in winter. Best to book. The open-air **Café Limbo** at Reynolds Yarraman (*Yarraman Rd, Wybong; tel: (02) 6543 8488; open weekends 1100–1500; $$*) has spectacular views, great salads and some mean desserts. **Rosemount Vineyard Restaurant** (*Rosemount Rd, Denman; tel: (02) 6547 2310; open Tue–Sun 1200–1400; $$*) serves a limited, but interesting menu (*best to book*), and cream teas from 1000. Indulge at **Roberts**, at the Pepper Tree vineyard (*Halls Rd, Pokolbin; tel: (02) 4998 7330; open daily lunch and dinner; $$$*). Run by Algerian-born Robert and his wife Sally, the cosy, wooden-beamed restaurant, adjoining an 1876 ironbark settler's cottage, offers truly excellent food such as wood-smoked quail and fresh black pasta with calamari.

What to try

The Blue Mountains has so far managed to resist the fast-food chain invasion and generally there's a strong leaning towards wholesome, organic 'slow food'. Bread is Leura's speciality, particularly sourdough, known locally as 'brickbread'. **Quinton's Bakery** (*179 The Mall; open daily 0730–1930*) offers a fine range of bread, gourmet sarnies and cakes.

Shops

Leura's high street (The Mall) abounds with art and crafty shops. Two fragrant, new-age shops to check out are **Moontree Studio** (*157 The Mall*) for beautifully scented candles, lanterns, hand-cut soaps and candleholders as big as cart wheels and the gloriously eclectic **Cinnamon Road** (*181 The Mall*) for similar fare plus beautiful wood crafts and mirrors. **Breewood** (*169 The Mall*) offers some upmarket ceramics and china. The **Leura Fine Woodwork Gallery** (*130 The Mall*) is an autumnal kaleidoscope of shiny woods from red cedar mirrors, to black wood clocks, sculptures and simple aboriginal art.

Katoomba offers all the gear you need for an active holiday – try **Summit Gear** (*88 Katoomba St*) for climbing, cycling and bushwalking togs, and the **Hatter's Shop** in the parallel street (*171 Lurline St*) for Akubra hats in every style.

Cinema

For the ultimate Blue Mountains experience without so much as a blister, catch *The Edge Movie* at the **Maxivision Cinema** (*Great Western Highway, Katoomba; tel: (02) 4782 8900*), which shows the mountain wilderness on giant screens daily, as well as the latest feature films.

National parks

For visitors from small, densely inhabited countries, such as Britain, one of the most striking features of Australia is the sheer vastness of space. With a total of 6.2 million people, New South Wales is one of the most heavily populated states, yet off the main coastal roads, you can feel as if you're the only person on the planet.

But this surplus of land does not mean that it is taken for granted. As far back as 1863, laws were passed in Tasmania to protect Australia's evocative landscape, with the first national park (**the Royal**) established south of Sydney in 1879. Since then, a protected status has been granted to more than 50 million hectares, encompassing over 3400 sites of particular interest for their wildlife and vegetation.

There are more than 70 national parks in NSW, taking in over 4 million hectares of land. Some of these are within the city of Sydney, such as the **Sydney Harbour National Park**, others are rugged wilderness areas, such as **Barrington Tops**.

Many national parks have marked walking trails and barbecue and picnic facilities; some of the larger ones have visitor's centres, cafés and campsites, but they are very low key and uncommercialised – you won't find McDonalds outlets and ice-cream vans. Very few national parks in NSW charge a fee, except for camping – notable exceptions are **Kosciuszko**, **Ku-ring-gai Chase** and **Jervis Bay**.

> " *I love a sunburnt country,*
> *A land of sweeping plains,*
> *Of ragged mountain ranges,*
> *Of droughts and flooding rains,*
> *I love her far horizons,*
> *I love her jewel sea,*
> *Her beauty and her terror,*
> *The wide brown land for me.* "

**Dorothea Mackellar, poet and
novelist,** *My Country* **(1911)**

The parks vary tremendously
in flora and fauna, from the
moist sub-tropical rainforests
in the north to the eerie alpine snow gums in the south.
However, whether you find yourself tiptoeing across the
tops of waterfalls, clambering over massive plank buttress
roots in a 6000-year-old rainforest or plunging into crystal-
clear coastal waters, the natural treasures of NSW parks
are not to be missed.

Here are a few to savour:

North of Sydney

Myall Lakes National Park, near Hawk's Nest. Sand dune
upon golden sand dune against a backdrop of mangrove
lakes (*see page 110*).

Boorganna Nature Reserve, 60km southwest of Port
Macquarie. An eerie, atmospheric rainforest surrounding
Rawson Falls with plentiful bird life (*see page 106*).

Dorrigo National Park, west of Coffs Harbour. A rainforest
listed as a World Heritage site (*see pages 126–127*).

South of Sydney

Kosciuszko National Park, Snowy Mountains. The
highest mountain in Australia plus stunning alpine scenery
(*see pages 140–141*).

Booderee National Park's Jervis Bay, 25km south of
Nowra. Spectacular white sandy beaches and plentiful
wildlife (*see page 138*).

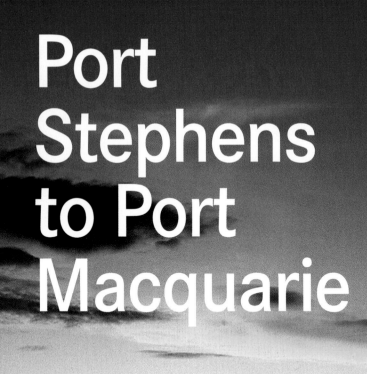

Port Stephens to Port Macquarie

Port Stephens and Port Macquarie are a far cry from high-rise blocks and disco lights. Their attractions are completely natural – beautiful surfing beaches, nearby national parks, an abundance of wildlife and flowers. They're the ultimate seaside playgrounds brimming with Australia's wild and wonderful treasures, sandy havens for those who want to fish, swim and sail whilst becoming acquainted with a dolphin or two.

BEST OF

Port Stephens to Port Macquarie

*Getting there: **By coach: Port Stephens Buses** run daily from Eddy Avenue, Central Station, Sydney (tel: (02) 4982 2940). **By train:** daily trains run to the nearest station, Wauchope (19km away), where a Countrylink bus service connects with Port Macquarie. **By coach:** several daily coach services run from Sydney, leaving from Eddy Avenue, Central Station including **McCafferty's** (tel: (02) 9212 3433; central reservations: 131 499; www.mccaffertys.com.au).*

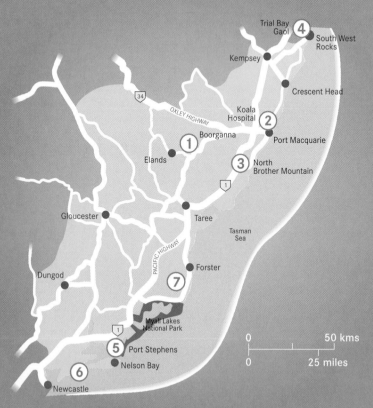

① Walk the walk

You could walk for the whole holiday and still find more wildflower-strewn tracks, more kangaroo-spotting trails, more yellow-tailed black-cockatoo haunts . . . there's not a single national park that disappoints but Boorganna, with its misty rainforest and crashing Rawson Falls is a must. **Page 106** The lighthouse to Town Beach Port Macquarie coastal walk is hard to beat. **Page 104**

② Kiss it better

Bush areas around Port Stephens and Port Macquarie are breeding habitats for koalas. They're easier to spot from October to February, when they're on the move in search of a mate. But if those sleepy little creatures are hiding away in the crook of a eucalyptus tree, head down to the Koala Hospital at Port Macquarie for a close-up of convalescing koalas on the mend. **Page 105**

③ See the sights

A view down from the summit of North Brother Mountain slots the watery jigsaw puzzle into place, showing how the complex natural irrigation system of waterways and lakes keeps the surrounding areas so incredibly lush. **Page 107**

④ Go to gaol

With its imposing granite walls, Trial Bay Gaol at South West Rocks conjures up eerie images of convicts looking longingly out through the barred windows to the freedom of the countryside beyond. The nearby Monument Trail bushwalk is one of the most beautiful in the area. **Page 107**

⑤ Flipping heck

If your only experience of dolphins is in a tank at the zoo, enjoy the true beauty of these sleek, intelligent animals roaming wild, riding the bow waves of the boats in Port Stephens. In migrating season, just beyond the harbour, you might even spot a humpback or southern right whale on its yearly trip to the tropics and back. **Page 108**

⑥ Cross the Sahara

It's easy to become blasé about NSW's beautiful beaches but Stockton Beach is superlative, a series of giant windblown dunes deposited on the shore over 6000 years ago. In fact, 'beach' seems a little tame when the other end is over 30km away, and the mobile sand mounds are marching steadily inland at a rate of 10m a year. **Page 109**

⑦ Say a prayer

You don't have to be religious to appreciate the natural splendour of this outdoor place of worship. The Green Cathedral, tucked away on the edge of the lake, with sand for a floor and palm trees for a roof, is a little piece of heaven right here on earth. **Page 111**

103

Tourist information

Port Macquarie Visitor Information Centre: *cnr Clarence & Hay Sts, Port Macquarie. Tel: (02) 6581 8000, toll free: 1800 025 935. Open Mon–Fri 0830–1700, weekends 0900–1600.*
Bulahdelah Visitors Centre: *cnr Pacific Hwy & Crawford St, Bulahdelah. Tel: (02) 4997 4981. E-mail: tourbglc@tpgi.com.au*
Port Stephens Visitors Centre: *Victoria Parade, Nelson Bay. Tel: 1800 808 900, website: www.portstephens. org.au. Open Mon–Fri 0900–1700, weekends 0900–1600.*

Port Macquarie

Founded as a penal colony in 1821 at the mouth of the Hastings River, Port Macquarie is one of the oldest towns in Australia, although historical buildings are few and far between. Today, it's a stunning combination of natural elements – splendid beaches, littoral rainforest, abundant wildlife (and man-made ones) – good restaurants, child-friendly attractions and adrenalin-pumping activities.

It's the ultimate holiday destination, without 'kiss-me-quick' tackiness, and a brilliant base for day-trips. Within an hour of Port (as it's known to the locals), you can tuck yourself away in a peaceful paradise of dense rainforest, tumbling waterfalls and national parks thronging with wildlife.

Appreciate the scenery from **the lighthouse** (south of the town) where the fabulous view confirms yet again that Australians are privileged people. It's prime whale-spotting

territory during the migration season and dolphins frolic here all year round. A soul-soothing, 2- to 3-hour **coastal walk** leads from the lighthouse back to Town Beach. Take the track off to the left at the Miner's Beach 0.8km sign, through the forest to a semicircle of near-deserted golden sand. Walking north involves a few rocky scrambles and detours onto the road, taking in several beaches along the way. The long **Shelly Beach** is a medley of Australian beach culture: young lads ride mountain bikes with boogie boards on their backs, kids bathe naked

in rock pools and families barbecue steaks the size of a cow.
Lighthouse beach, down Matthew Flinders Drive, can
be explored by **camel safari** (*tel: (02) 6583 7650/mobile
0412 566 333; $$*).

A must-see Port sight is the **Koala Hospital** (*Lord St; open
daily; donation*), if only for its 'aaa-aah' factor. Dedicated to
the rescue of injured koalas and their release back into the
wild, the hospital's eucalyptus enclosure usually houses
around 8 animals (up to 40 after bushfires). Koalas are
notoriously difficult to spot, so aim for feeding time (*1500
–1530*) when hospital favourites such as Pebbles, whose
jaw was broken in a road accident, descend
for their hand-fed rations. If you're heading
north for bushwalking in the national parks,
a trip to the **Sea Acres Rainforest Centre**
(*Pacific Drive; open daily 0900–1630; $$*), a
rare area of coastal rainforest, will give you
a taste of what to look out for, such as the
walking stick palm, strangler fig and python
trees. Volunteer rangers run guided tours,
pointing out birds and their nests, such as the
spectacled monarch and the brush turkey.

> **"** *The biggest threat to koalas
> is Man – we run them over,
> let our dogs loose on them
> and bulldoze their habitat
> for roads and housing
> developments.* **"**
> **Koala Hospital volunteer**

Activities

For those who want to do more than lie on a beach, there's
plenty of activities to choose from. The **Port Marina
Complex** (*opposite McDonald's on Park St*) houses
Graham Seers bike hire (*tel: (02) 6583 2333; closed Sun;
$$*); **Port Macquarie Dive Centre** (*tel: (02) 6583 8483;
$$$*) and **Hastings River Boat Hire** (*tel: (02) 6583 8811;
$$–$$$*). The **Town Wharf**, north of Town Beach, is the
booking and departure point for boat-based activities such
as scenic river and dolphin-watching cruises: try **M V** *Port
Venture* (*tel: (02) 6583 3058/after hours 018 65 6522; $$*),
Waterbus Everglade Tours (*tel: (02) 6582 5009; $$*)
and **Fanta-Sea II** (*tel: 015 256 742/after hours (02) 6582
2037; $$*). **Odyssey Charters** (*tel: 0412 288 116/(02)
6586 3132; $$$*) and **Sea Quest** (*tel: (02) 6583 3463; $$$*)
provide reef- or game-fishing charters, whilst **Port Water
Sports** (*tel: 0412 234 509; $$$*) offers parasailing and
speedboat cruises.

Out and about around Port Macquarie

*Take the spectacular drive **southwest** up to the sleepy village of Comboyne (turn left off the Oxley highway 32km from Port Macquarie) along a steep and winding forested road. You eventually spill out onto a fertile green plateau, reminiscent of the English countryside in spring.*

Continue on to **Boorganna Nature Reserve** (*free*), which is nature at its best. Despite partial logging of the area during the 1950s, many of the surviving trees are thousands of years old. The 2.7km walk down to the bottom of **Rawson Falls** is a misty, fragrant, almost eerie trail, weaving between enormous plank buttresses, brush boxes, water gums and the smooth white trunks of pigeon berry ash. At the bottom of the fall is a freezing-cold rock pool – only for the very brave – which nestles in a tranquil valley of bird's-nest ferns. A further 15-minute drive takes you to **Ellenborough Falls**

(85km from Port Macquarie), the longest single-drop waterfall in the southern hemisphere. It's a great place for picnicking and meandering bush walks.

A trip **south** from Port Macquarie towards Laurieton takes you past Christmas Bell Plain, which is a carpet of red Christmas Bell flowers around December and January. For more flora and fauna, turn off to the **Kattang Nature Reserve** (*free*) at Dunbogan. An undemanding 2km circular walk called the Flower Bowl takes you through small pockets of rainforest and wildflower heaths, affording panoramic views south to **Diamond Head** and north to Port Macquarie along the way. August and September see the most wildflowers in bloom, whilst June and July attract a variety of birds. Further south on the coastal road is Diamond Head, yet another wondrous white stretch of sand. If you've yet to see a kangaroo at close quarters, then head to the camping site here where, amongst the weekenders pitching their tents, Skippy and his relatives are out in force. There's a visitors' information centre (*Diamond Head Rest Area, Crowdy Bay National Park, Laurieton; tel: 018 474 679; open 0800–2000*) with maps of headland walks. Back towards Laurieton is **North Brother Mountain** (off Ocean Drive), where look-out platforms offer an eagle-eye view of the labyrinth of waterways, rivers and lakes. The scenery is 360-degree magnificent with views over Queen's Lake, the mountain's other siblings, Middle and South Brother, the Camden Haven River and the broad sweep of Crowdy Bay, plus the many hang-gliders who use the summit as a launch pad.

North of Port is **Crescent Head**, one of the best surfing beaches along this part of the coast, with stunning views (turn right off the Pacific Highway just before Kempsey). Further north still is the partly ruined **Trial Bay Gaol** (*open daily 0900–1700; $$*), standing majestically on the South West Rocks headland, empty windows silhouetted against the sky. Built as a reform prison in the 1880s, it was also home to German internees during World War I. It was partly demolished in 1922. You can wander through Cell Block A where a couple of the 4m x 2m cells have life-size dummies recreating prison life. There's also a small museum detailing the crimes of the various inmates from horse-stealing Scots to drink-pinching Englishmen. After visiting the gaol, head along the beautiful **Monument Trail**, where a hillside monument commemorates the Germans who died during their internment. Sea eagles duck and dive over the water, butterflies dart backwards and forwards and the trail criss-crosses beautiful heathland with views over both sides of the headland.

107

Getting there: turn off the Pacific Highway following signs to Gladstone, then South West Rocks.

The best beach

Ask a surfer what makes great surf and be prepared to crack open a VB and listen awhile. It's the swell, the sand, the offshore wind, the headland. A combination of factors give each beach its own unique qualities and defects, which mean the best surfing beach in the state can be brilliant one day and dire the next.

Port Stephens

Five escaped convicts from Sydney were the first Europeans to live in the Port Stephens area after they were shipwrecked in 1790. Taken in by Worimi aborigines, they probably thought they'd swum to paradise.

Port Stephens, a large, sheltered natural harbour, enjoys stunning beaches and scenery and the company of many pods of bottle-nose dolphins. Today it's a weekend water playground for Sydneysiders and a great spot to relax whilst planning the next step of your tour.

Nelson Bay, on the southern side, is the largest town, the most 'commercialised' of the surrounding resorts, although there's not a high-rise block in sight. But forget the town: those smooth, beaky dolphins and seasonal visiting whales are Nelson Bay's *raison d'être*: a whole armada of boats runs **dolphin-watching tours** ranging from a couple of hours to all-day excursions. Derek's Dolphin Cruises (*$$–$$$*) are friendly, informal affairs with boom netting thrown in – a wet and wild ride in a giant net off the back of the boat. More upmarket is the luxury yacht cruise, *Advance II* (*$$$*), but there's a myriad of options: barbecue lunches, island visits, twilight dinners, trips to Hawk's Nest on the northern side. From January to April, Nelson Bay is a prime spot for **game fishing** (*$$$*). Locals claim the Port Stephens' exceptionally deep water makes for the best marlin fishing in the world.

> " *When I think 'beach holiday', I think Australia. There's a wonderfully wild element to our beaches which really sets them apart. The surf's different, the sand much softer and finer, and the water's a singular colour.* "
>
> **Sabrina Bratton, NSW Businesswoman,**
> *Places in the Heart*

All bookings for water activities can be made at the **Boat Hire** floating office at D'Albora Marinas (*tel: (02) 4984 3843*).

For waterbabes, the marine sanctuary between **Nelson Head** and **Fly Point** offers excellent snorkelling and scuba diving. Port Stephens is a diver's heaven as it is surrounded by underwater shipwrecks. **Pro Dive** (*D'Albora*

Marina; tel: (02) 4981 4331; $$$) runs courses for all levels. Back on land, bushwalkers can stretch their legs with a walk up to the volcanic rock peninsula, **Tomaree Head**, or stroll over **Fingal Spit** at low tide, a narrow sand bank connecting the glorious Fingal Beach (off Marine Drive), a fantastic surfing spot, to the rocky reef of **Point Stephens** (once across, you might have to wait for the next low tide!). The energetic can hire a bike (*see page 113*) and explore Port Stephens' many scenic cycleways.

(*see page 113*)

Sun worshippers are spoilt for choice around Nelson Bay. **Little Beach**, north of the lighthouse, is a safe, child-friendly cove. Gan Gan Rd gives access to beaches south of the lighthouse: **One Mile Beach** offers the best surf, whilst **Samurai Beach** (near Bardot's Nude Village) gives nudists a chance to let it all hang out. However, the must-visit beach is **Stockton** (turn left down James Paterson St), which embodies the difference between 'sand' and 'Sahara'. Golden dunes, 30m high, stretch as far as the eye can see, undulating desert-like towards Newcastle for 33km. A track just past James Paterson Rd allows you access for a drive on the beach if you're in a 4WD. **Horizon Safaris** (*tel: 018 681 600; $$–$$$*) run 4WD dune adventures, **Sahara Trails** offers horseback coastal rides (*tel: 015 290 340; $$–$$$*).

109

Great Lakes and beyond

*More natural attractions await on the north side of Port Stephens, including **Myall Lakes National Park**, which runs along the coast from Hawk's Nest to Seal Rocks.*

It's a network of coastal lakes, golden beaches and wild scenery with spectacular multi-hued swamps and trees growing straight out of the water. In spring the area is dotted with wild roses and white lilies. **Mungo Brush** rainforest walking trail (badly signposted – far right-hand side of Mungo Brush campsite) is an undemanding palm-shaded trail which meanders down to the edge of Bombah Broadwater. If you're there at dusk, keep your eyes open for a flying fox or ring-tailed possums. On the other side of the road, pale sands and Pacific breakers offer beach fishing and surfing.

Getting there

Take the Pacific Highway north, entering the park from the south via Tea Gardens and Hawks Nest, or turn off at Bulahdelah and catch the ferry over (it runs every half an hour 0800–1800 daily and takes about 3 minutes) at Bombah Point.

Further treasures lie along the **Lakes Way**, an 85km scenic coastal road, just beyond Bulahdelah. A curiosity worth visiting, but only in a 4WD, is the **Grandis Tree** (turn left down Stoney Creek Rd). At 76m high, this Eucalyptus Grandis Flooded Gum is the tallest tree in the southern hemisphere. It's 400 years old, with a circumference of 10m. Make it your picnic stop – the 6km rough road means you'll want to stop more than the 20 seconds it takes to admire the tree.

After a further 15km you reach the turn to **Seal Rocks** (11km down a reasonable road), a popular surfing area around a rocky headland, with a backdrop of thickly wooded sandstone cliffs. A wave-crashing 10-minute stroll up to Sugarloaf Point lighthouse offers a view over a coastline of deserted crescents of pale sand down to Hawk's Nest. For a day out on calmer waters, nearby **Smith's Lake** is a good spot for families. Catamarans, canoes, windsurfers and motor boats can be hired from the colonial-style **Frothy Coffee Boatshed** on the lakeshore (*tel: (02) 6554 4202; $$*). For a place of worship, the outdoor **Green Cathedral** at Tiona Park must be one step closer to heaven. Situated on the shore of Wallis Lake amongst lush palm trees and ferns, this quirky, consecrated venue has rough-hewn log pews, a stone altar, a sandy floor and a palm-frond roof.

More messing about on the river takes place on a large scale at **Forster-Tuncurry**, twin towns situated where Wallis Lake meets the sea. Strings of boatsheds along Little St offer a wide range of activities from combined 4WD rainforest and lake cruises to boat hire, snorkelling and diving. The **Aussie Boatshed** (*11 Little St; tel: (02) 6554 5255*) is the place to go for diving with grey nurse sharks around Seal Rocks, whilst the **Tikki Boatshed** (*15 Little St; tel: (02) 6554 6321*) knows a man who can for every conceivable tour.

Twitchers will love the **'satay and sunset' birdwatching cruise** (*tel: (02) 6554 4168; $$–$$$*) run by local nature author Libby Buhrich. Her knowledge and gourmet cooking skills make this journey through shallow bays and hidden inlets a delightful combination of majestic birds and top-notch tucker. She also runs birdwatching breakfast walks around Smith's Lakes.

111

One for sorrow

It sounds like a typical Aussie yarn, but during nesting season (August–October) the black and white Australian Magpie is renowned for dive-bombing people, occasionally attacking the 'intruder's' head with its beak or claws. In known magpie areas, Australians resort to carrying an open umbrella, wearing bicycle helmets or sewing a pair of eyes on the back of a hat because magpies are less likely to swoop if you look at them!

Eating out

Nelson Bay restaurants

Inner Lighthouse Tea Room

Little Beach. Open daily 1000–1600. Situated in a restored 1875 lighthouse, this is one of the prettiest spots for coffee and cake with fabulous views out to sea.

Kaleidoscope

Nelson Towers Arcade. Tel: (02) 4981 3773. Open breakfast– lunch. $. Light bites – pumpkin soup, Mediterranean focaccia, gourmet sandwiches – on an upstairs panoramic balcony.

Red Bellies

Nelson Lodge Motel, 1 Government Rd. Tel: (02) 4981 1705. Open daily from 1800. $$$. Seafood and steak, emu and kangaroo, with 'bush tucker' flavours such as Illawarra plum salsa and wattleseed sauce.

Robs on the boardwalk

D'Albora Marinas. Tel: (02) 4984 4444. Open daily breakfast– dinner. $$. A mellow waterfront spot for robust breakfasts and mod Oz lunches and dinners with delights such as ravioli of plump scallops and blue-eyed cod with truffle-infused mash.

Rocklobster

D'Albora Marina, Nelson Bay. Tel: (02) 4981 1813. Open daily. $$–$$$. This bright, light restaurant serves exquisite fish dishes such as prawns in beer batter and red Thai fish curry on an outdoor terrace with beautiful views. Licensed and BYO.

Port Macquarie restaurants and cafés

Café 66

Clarence St. Tel: (02) 6583 2484. Open Tue–Sun, breakfast–dinner. $$. Busy and buzzing, this friendly café serves tasty Italian fare with a flourish. BYO.

Crays fish restaurant

74 Clarence St. Tel: (02) 6583 7885. Open daily for lunch, Mon–Sat for dinner. $$$. It's not cheap but delicate sauces (champagne, lemon butter – on the freshest fish: baby snapper, dory, lobster) transform good into great.

Family Buffet restaurant

14 Clarence St. Tel: (02) 6584 9838. Open daily lunch and dinner. $. Despite the uninspiring name, this eat-as-much-as-you-want diner with oriental, seafood, salad and roasts is great value and good, if not gourmet.

Noodle World

1/72 Clarence St. Tel: (02) 6583 9838. Open Mon–Sat for lunch, daily for dinner. $. Excellent Malay cuisine to eat in or take away.

Pottsy's Place

1 Hay St. Tel: (02) 6583 4941. Open daily from 1800, lunch Sun–Fri. $$. This lively rustic restaurant on the sea front serves dainty dishes of kangaroo, crocodile and venison, as well as seafood and steak. Licensed or BYO.

Out and about

Blue Poles Café

*Byabarra, on the road to Comboyne.
Tel: (02) 6587 1167. Open Wed–Sun
0900–1700. $.* This friendly café-
gallery is a place where people play
the piano, take drawing lessons,
sample the owner's fantastic chocolate
cake or linger on the terrace watching
the birds dance in a garden. Bliss.

Fat Ant Café

*32 Wharf St, Forster. Tel: (02) 6555
3444. Open daily in summer lunch and
dinner; in winter Tue–Sun for lunch,
Wed–Sat for dinner.* A fun, family-
friendly place with a corrugated-iron
shack bar, a veranda overlooking the
lake and simple, tasty nosh.

The Udder Cow Café

*Cnr Comboyne and Main Sts.Tel: (02)
6550 4188. Open Wed–Mon 0900–
1700. $.* Frothy coffee, tasty snacks
and black-and-white cow jugs, mugs,
teapots and flowerpots to remind you
that you're in cattle-grazing country.

What to try

Stockton is one of the best fishing
beaches in NSW, and whatever is in
season will grace restaurant menus in
the area. Look out for jewfish (Feb–Apr),
bream (Apr–May), whiting and dusky
flathead (Oct–Feb). Port Stephens
oysters are also particularly good.

Shops

Port Macquarie has two shopping
malls with high street chains and
department stores: Settlement City
north of the town centre and Port
Central on Clarence St. **Nelson Bay
Sports** (*77 Victoria Parade, Nelson
Bay; tel: (02) 4981 2333*) is a one-
stop sports equipment shop hiring
out everything from snorkelling gear
to bikes, roller blades, fishing rods
and body boards.

Nightlife

Nelson Bay's RSL club (*Shoal
Bay Rd*) offers live music, pool
competitions, karaoke and discos,
whilst **Port Macquarie's RSL**
(*tel: (02) 6580 2300*) at Settlement
City has live bands on Friday and
Saturday. **Goochies** (*2/72 Clarence
St, Port Macquarie*) is an elegant
wine bar for pre- and post-dinner
drinking, something of a rarity in
Australia. Forster's **Fat Ant Café**
(*see above*) has a live band and DJ
on Thursday, a disco on Friday and
live jazz every second Sunday.

Australia's wildlife

Much of Australia's wildlife is unique. Isolated from the rest of the world for over 55 million years, marsupials such as wombats and koalas were able to flourish, unthreatened by highly developed mammals. Three hundred of the country's 750 bird species are unique to Australia. Walks in national parks are like a stroll through a living zoo, punctuated with cheeky kookaburras cackling in the trees, eastern grey kangaroos bounding across pathways and brightly coloured parrots fluttering out of the bushes.

Here's what you're most likely to see:

Bottle-nose dolphins. These warm-blooded mammals can hold their breath for as long as seven minutes as they plunge to depths of 300m. They eventually need to surface to breathe through their blowhole.

Cockatoos. The two species you're most likely to see are the yellow-tailed black cockatoo and the sulphur-crested cockatoo, which is white with a yellow crest. Both tend to fly in large groups.

Eastern grey kangaroo. Second in size only to the red kangaroo, you're very likely to see one on your travels, probably with a joey hanging out of its pouch. Take it easy at dusk – those roo bars on cars are there for a reason.

Tip

Early settlers described kangaroos as 'mice the size of greyhounds'.

Emus. These large flightless birds are terrible thieves, so hold onto your picnic if they're around.

Galah. This pink-breasted, grey-winged bird is a common sight in national parks near Sydney, the Hunter Valley and Blue Mountains.

Koala. These nocturnal animals sleep for up to 18 hours a day and feed at night on eucalyptus trees, making them very difficult to see in the wild.

Kookaburra. This large brown-and-white kingfisher has a distinctive cackling call, and preys on snakes, insects, lizards and worms for food.

Rosellas. The crimson rosella is red with purple wings and tail, whilst the eastern rosella is multi-hued with a red head, yellow breast and blue-and-green tail. Keep an eye out, too, for belligerent, noisy, brightly coloured rainbow lorikeets.

Whales. Humpback whales can be seen along NSW's coast, migrating north to Queensland's Great Barrier Reef in late May to July to mate and give birth to their young. From September to early November, they head to the food-rich waters of the Antarctic.

From Coffs Harbour to Byron Bay

The coast offers the surfing paradise of Byron Bay, vibrating to the sound of the bongos and the didgeridoo. The hinterland delivers eucalyptus forests and fertile plains, dotted with sleepy old timber towns.

FROM COFFS HARBOUR TO BYRON BAY

From Coffs Harbour to Byron Bay

Getting there: **Byron Bay:** *Byron Bay is just off the Pacific Highway. There is a daily train from Sydney via Coffs Harbour. McCafferty's and Greyhound buses run daily services to Byron Bay via Port Macquarie and Coffs Harbour.* **Nimbin:** *Driving to Nimbin via Bangalow and Lismore is the easiest, via the Channon is more scenic. Several tours run from Byron (* see page 16 *). Nimbin shuttle bus runs daily from Byron 1000, returning 1430 (* tel: (02) 6687 2007 *).*

Nimbin

Nightcap
National Park

Byron Bay

①

②

Lismore

44

BRUXNER HIGHWAY

Ballina

91

1

Evans Head

PACIFIC HIGHWAY

30

Maclean

⑥ Grafton

Tasman
Sea

Dorrigo

⑤

Bellingen

④

③ Coffs
Harbour

0   50 kms

0   25 miles

① Life of Byron

The tourist literature claims that Byron Bay is 'one of the few places in the world where you can sit amongst native wildflowers and grasses on the edge of the rainforest and listen to a whale breathe'. When there's no wind, that's true. What more incentive do you need to visit this laid-back, surfing mecca of the north coast? **Pages 120–121**

② Get real

A stroll along Nimbin's high street feels as if you've stumbled back into the 1960s. Populated with environmentalists, spiritualists, and just about every other politically correct -ist, this alternative, rainbow-coloured capital of Australia lends itself to lazy café lunches, surreal conversations and weird and wonderful shops. **Page 123**

③ Dive deep

Only an oxygen tank stands between you and underwater paradise. Nothing can prepare you for the stillness and sheer abundance of tropical and temperate fish life that surrounds the Solitary Islands in the marine reserve by Coffs Harbour. If you want to swim with the sharks, this is your chance. Come to Coffs in early August for the festivities surrounding the town's premier horse race, the Gold Cup. **Pages 124–125**

④ Bellingen

Maybe it's the soporific blend of classy craft shops ripe for browsing, the quaint olde worlde buildings and the luxuriant landscape of the nearby Promised Land, but this sleepy little town makes you want to sit on a wall, kicking your heels and dreaming a while. If you've still got work on your mind, you won't have for long. Come on the third Saturday of the month for the large country market, August for the three-day jazz festival (*infoline: (02) 6655 9345*), in October

for the Global Festival of traditional, classical and contemporary music and dance. **Page 126**

⑤ Dorrigo National Park

As long ago as 1893, a botanist said of Dorrigo 'Looking up and down the face of the Dorrigo Mountain, the vegetation is full of interest'. Today, as a World Heritage Site rainforest, it is one of the most rewarding national parks to visit, with vine-strewn trails over cascading falls and views over the lush Bellingen Valley. Come in the school holidays to join one of the Rainforest Centre's excellent guided walks. **Pages 126–127**

⑥ Festival of flowers

Most Sydneysiders' response to the mention of Grafton, a pretty town on the banks of the Clarence River, is 'Isn't that where you change buses for Byron Bay?' But to pass it by, especially when the jacaranda trees are in flower, is to miss a little inland gem, with graceful old buildings, tree-lined streets and courteous, old-fashioned hospitality. Come the last weekend of October for the Jacaranda Festival. **Page 127**

Tourist information

Coffs Harbour: *cnr Rose Ave and Marcia St. Tel: (02) 6652 1522/toll free 1800 025 650.* **Dorrigo Rainforest Centre**: *Dorrigo National Park. Tel: (02) 6657 2309.* **Clarence River Tourist Association**: *cnr Spring St & Pacific Highway, Grafton. Tel: (02) 6643 4677.* **Byron Visitor Centre**: *Jonson St, by the railway station. Tel: (02) 6685 8050. www.byronbay.com.* **Nimbin Ecotourist Connexion**: *80 Cullen St. Tel: (02) 6689 1764. Open Mon–Fri 1200–1700, Sat–Sun 1200–1400.*

Byron Bay I

Named by Captain Cook as he sailed past in 1770, Byron Bay was, until recently, home to several industries. Originally a stopping-off point for cedar fellers in the early 19th century, it became a centre for the dairy trade and butter production by the 1880s, then sand mining in the 1930s and whaling in the 1950s.

Recently, it has found its niche as the alternative, 'new age' NSW holiday spot for the young and trendy. Surfers flock here for the excellent waves around Cape Byron, whilst others revel in the laid-back, patchouli-perfumed atmosphere. Once exclusively the domain of backpackers, Byron's repertoire is more sophisticated these days, with excellent restaurants, shops and a myriad of activities from hang-gliding to trapeze. Holiday elation hangs in the air, but there's no sense – yet – of commercial exploitation. High-rise buildings are banned, there are no fast-food chains, but as thousands of visitors cram in alongside the 8000 permanent residents, you can't help wondering how long that will last.

Beaches

There's something about the wildness of Byron's beaches that makes you want to fling your clothes in the air and turn a series of cartwheels. And should you want to do so, the 7km **Tallow** beach, south of the cape, is 'clothing optional', recently joined by **Belongil** beach to the north.

> " *Even if you're not into all this new age stuff, you can't help being sucked in – there's something magical about the place. I was talking to this guy with the most amazing piercing blue eyes and I thought . . . I hope there's no one here who's into mind bending.* "
>
> **Teresa Valentine, first-time English visitor to Byron**

The **Pass** and **Watego** offer some of the best surfing on the east coast, whilst a natural lagoon often forms at **Clarks** beach, making it safe for young families. **Main** beach is popular with kite fliers who dive bomb their flexifoils over the heads of the sunseekers.

As in many of the east coast towns, the best things to do aren't so much about formal sightseeing as enjoying Byron's natural features. It's the most easterly point in Australia, so be the first to see the **sunrise** from Cape Byron and drink the dawn in with a champagne breakfast. Or brunch at the **Beach Café** (*see page 128*) on Clarks Beach before **walking** the 3.5km lighthouse circuit. Anticlockwise is easiest on the legs – a track to the right (about 150m before the northern end of Clarks) to Captain Cook Lookout leads through the rainforest to the tip of **Cape Byron**, top whale-spotting point from May to August. The return journey via Wategos beach and Palm Valley encompasses spectacular scenery. If you want the panorama without the exercise, drive up to Cape Byron. *The area around the lighthouse is open daily, 0800–1730.*

Other close-to-nature excursions include **horse riding** (*$$*) on the beach (**Byron Beach Rides**, *tel: (02) 6684 7499*; **Pegasus Park Equestrian Centre**, *tel: (02) 6687 1446*); **sea kayaking** (*$$*) with curious dolphins who pop their noses up and swim alongside (**Byron Bay Ocean Kayaking**, *tel: (02) 6685 7651*); and **snorkelling** and **diving** (*$$$*) at the Julian Rocks Marine Reserve, 2.5km off shore (**Bayside Scuba**, *cnr Lawson and Fletcher Sts; tel: (02) 6685 8333/ toll free 1800 243 483*). If you're going to try standing on those slippery little sucker surfboards (*$$*), Byron is the place to do it. The instructors at **Swell Surf Co** (*tel: (02) 6685 5352*) are slightly more expensive than their competitors, but guarantee small groups. Other options are **East Coast Surf School** (*tel: (02) 6685 5989*) and **Byron Bay Surf School** (*tel: 1800 707 274*).

Byron Bay II

Alternative times

Byron Bay is the centre of all that is spiritual, soulful and downright whacky. If you need to find yourself, the new age shop **Focus** (*cnr Marvell and Jonson Sts*) is a good place to start, as it sells everything from poetry, dream catchers and joss sticks. It's here you'll find the contacts for alternative therapies, singing workshops, gibberish sessions (really!), silent retreats *et al.* **Osho's House** (*1/30 Carlyle St; tel: (02) 6685 6792*), where the sign at the front door reads 'Step inside and leave your shoes and mind behind' offers soul-soothing flotation tanks, reflexology, tarot-card readings and aura soma sessions within its tranquil walls.

Flying high

The opportunities to fly high in Byron are many, even without the pot. For unparalleled views, fly over Byron Lighthouse in a two-seater plane, then glide back with the engine off with **Byron Power Gliding Club** (*tel: (02) 6684 7627; $$$*); or forget the mechanics and go tandem hang-gliding with **Joe Scott, Byron Bay Hang-gliding Club** (*tel: (02) 6684 3711/ 0415 717 141; $$$*). The action takes place around Cape Byron and nearby Lennox Head, depending on the wind, so book early as the right conditions might take a few days. It's a unique way to see the scenery as the wind whistles past and you fly above the birds, looking down on the beach (and the road!).

And if that's not exciting enough, turn yourself into a trapeze artiste in the safe hands of the **Circus School** at Byron Bay Beach Club (*Bayshore Drive; tel: (02) 6685 8000; $*). In just two hours, you'll have learned to swing from one trapeze to the other (with a safety net!), right into the arms of your co-artiste. Sheer elation. The complex also houses a nine-hole golf course and tennis courts.

Out and about around Byron Bay

Nimbin

A stroll through Nimbin is a surreal experience of facial tattoos, beards you could climb up, tie-dye clothes and the smell of marijuana. It's been the alternative capital of Australia since 1973, when a myriad of politically correct groups came here for the Aquarius festival. Communal living in harmony with the land is its mission, and the residents have been heavily involved in environmental protests. Many people come here to fill up on drugs, and you don't have to be Inspector Clouseau to find those. But even as a chemical virgin, the shops and cafés with colourful characters make it an interesting place to be. Don't miss the off-the-wall **Nimbin Museum** (*Cullen St; tel: (02) 6689 1123; open daily, no fixed hours; $*). It's almost a stream of consciousness with psychedelic 'exhibits' ranging from camper vans, environmental articles and informative 'Say Know to Drugs' section. The café's list of rules ranging from 'Let every one say their piece in whatever language they want' to 'put the scissors back' best sums up their approach to tolerant living.

Nightcap National Park

Created after Nimbin's environmental protesters successfully forced the government to halt further logging of the rainforests, Nightcap National Park is listed as a World Heritage Site. Take a slow drive up to **Mount Nardi** (12km) within the park: the long-nosed potoroo, pademelons (which resemble a big rat) and birdlife are extremely plentiful. Walking trails lead from the summit, although some are overgrown and peter out in places.

For the most scenic swim hole imaginable, head to the tumbling **Protestor's Falls** (access from the Channon, dirt road) which cascade over the rocks, tucked away in a palm-filled gorge amongst bird's nest ferns and huge rainforest trees.

Getting there: there are various entrances to Nightcap National Park. Mount Nardi is 12km northeast of Nimbin via Newton Drive.

Coffs Harbour

Head honcho of the banana-growing region and one of the largest towns on NSW's coast, Coffs Harbour isn't quaint, but it certainly offers variety. Set around a man-made harbour between inland subtropical rainforests and golden coastal beaches, Coffs is the place to come for an active, sporty holiday with good food and interesting day-trips. It can be a little soulless, with large shopping malls and out-of-town restaurant complexes, but the harbour area and Coffs Promenade on the edge of the creek are pleasant spots, and it's a brilliant base for exploring the rest of the region.

Getting active

For information on every activity from cruises, horse riding, deep-sea fishing, parasailing and 4WD trips, call in at the **Marina Booking Office** (*near Muttonbird Island; tel: (02) 6651 4612*). Here are some of the highlights:

Diving $$$

Solitary Islands Marine Park just north of Coffs offers some of the best diving on the NSW coast. It's here that tropical waters and cooler currents cross, which means that diverse marine life, from grey nurse sharks, blue tang tropical fish, sea turtles and plate corals, inhabits this underwater world. Snorkelling tours are nearly as rewarding. **Jetty Dive Centre** (*398 High St; tel: (02) 6651 1611*) runs snorkelling tours and a variety of PADI dive courses.

The Big Banana

Australians seem to have a strange penchant for huge landmarks: Coffs Harbour has the enormous Big Banana marking the entrance to a theme park, Goulburn in the south has the 15.2m-high Big Merino, as a reminder of the area's importance in wool production, and Port Macquarie has the huge fibreglass Big Bull at a dairy farm/children's tourist attraction.

Kayaking and canoeing $$

A 3-hour kayaking tour: **Coffs Sea Kayaking** (*tel: (02) 6658 0850*) is a good way to see dolphins, sea turtles and manta rays up close, with a stop for breakfast at a secluded cove. A less strenuous option is to hire a canoe or dinghy to explore the backwaters of Coffs Creek: **Promenade Leisure Hire** (*Coffs Promenade; tel: (02) 66511 1032; open daily 0900–1600; also hires out bikes*).

Walking

The glorious walks around Coffs include **Muttonbird Island** for a splendid – if windy – view over the harbour. Unfortunately, the muttonbirds burrow underground, so you're only likely to see them during August nights when they're flying back to breed here from southeast Asia. There's also a 6km relaxing stroll along **Coffs Creek** (starting from Coffs St), which links the Botanic Garden to Coffs Promenade and the Porpoise Pool, leading over mangrove boardwalks.

Whalewatching $$

Coffs claims to be the 'number one' whale-watching spot from June to October. Whether it's better than its other rivals along the coast is a matter of opinion, but a cruise is a lovely way to spend half a day, with a bit of breaching and pec slapping thrown in. Try the **Pacific Explorer**, which runs sailboat tours (*tel: 0418 663 815*), or **Spirit of Coffs Harbour** (*tel: (02) 6650 0155*), which also runs summer cruises around Solitary Islands.

Whitewater rafting and skydiving $$$

The Nymboida River in Dorrigo's hinterland offers some of the best whitewater rafting in NSW, with the added bonus of rainforest scenery. Trips range from one-day excursions to two- to four-day trips with wilderness camping. Aficionados should head for the swirling Gwydir River in summer, when water crashes down from an upstream dam; book through **Wildwater Adventures** (*tel: (02) 6653 4469*). Skydiving can be arranged with **Coffs City Skydivers** (*tel: (02) 6651 1167*).

Out and about around Coffs Harbour

Beach life

Coffs Harbour beaches are lovely, but seclusion-seekers should head north out of town. A right turn off the highway between Coffs and Woolgoolga should take you to a near-deserted beach. Sandy Beach is a good choice for families as the surf is usually placid, and as one local says, 'If there are more than 30 people here, we think it's crowded'.

Bellingen

Signposted off the Pacific Highway.

Bellingen should be a sleepy backwater, but it infiltrates the consciousness by virtue of its low-level tourism, jazz festivals and strong arts tradition. It's the perfect place to spend an afternoon 'fossicking' in some of the best craft shops in NSW having a coffee in one of the quaint cafés. If you have time, drive out towards the delightfully named **Promised Land** (via Gleniffer), on the banks of the Never Never River. The locals head here on hot days, for a refreshing, if freezing, swim in spring-fed water holes. The area is superbly lush, dotted with jacaranda trees in the spring and home to one famous resident – **David Helfgott**, the musical genius and subject of the film *Shine*, obviously not too troubled by curious visitors, judging by the name sign outside his house.

Red gold

Loggers opened up the Bellingen Valley in the 1840s for the lucrative red cedars known as 'red gold'. By the end of the century, the red cedars were almost extinct and the inhabitants turned to dairy farming. Although the Dorrigo plateau was cleared for cattle and potato crops, the precious rainforest was saved because the slopes were deemed too steep to clear.

Dorrigo National Park

60km from Coffs Harbour, via Bellingen and Waterfall Way.

A scenic drive southwest of Coffs Harbour climbing the aptly named Waterfall Way leads to Dorrigo, one of NSW's most outstanding national parks, encompassing both a high, cool plateau and steep rugged escarpment. World Heritage listed since 1986 for its magnificent rainforests, the park has paths overgrown with vines, where bird's nest ferns cling like crowns to huge buttress trunks, a feast for the senses. **The Skywalk**, a boardwalk suspended over the trees, offers

a rare view down onto the rainforest canopy, against a backdrop of flashes of colourful plummage. The 5.8km subtropical rainforest **Wonga Wonga walk** is one of the most picturesque, with 600-year-old yellow carabeens, strangler figs, and the cool Crystal Shower and Terania waterfalls.

Grafton

Pacific Highway.

Many people pass by this rural town in their hurry to reach Byron Bay but there are two excellent reasons for making a detour to Grafton. First, mid October to mid November, this riverside town is a stunning haze of purple jacaranda trees. Secondly, it is dotted with fine examples of colonial architecture, shaded by enormous old fig trees.

A historical walk (map available from the tourist office) starts from Victoria St, taking in the imposing, 1880s' **courthouse**, the 1930s' **Anglican cathedral** and the wrought-iron verandas of the **Roche** and **Crown** hotels. Fitzroy St is home to the Grafton **Regional Art Gallery** (*No 158*) in the beautiful 1880s' Prentice House (*open Tue– Sun 1000–1600, donation*), which specialises in drawings, whilst further along, **Schaeffer House** (*No 190*) contains the regional museum (*open Tue–Thur and Sun 1300–1600; $*) run by enthusiastic volunteers who will guide you through the Aladdin's cave of local history. Nearby **See Park** is a purple palette of jacaranda trees. The **Jacaranda Festival** begins on the last Saturday in October until the first weekend in November. The town's inhabitants go mad on Jacaranda Thursday, when floats hit the streets, bands play in every pub, and shops, banks and public buildings in **Prince St** turn into forums for would-be Spice Girls, Rocky Horror shows and Elvis pretenders.

Restaurants and cafés

Bellingen

Carriageway Café

75 Hyde St. Tel: (02) 6655 1672. Open daily 0800–1800. $. Huge portions of toast, doorstopper sandwiches, table-sized steaks and very friendly service.

Cool Creek Café

5 Church St. Tel: (02) 6655 1886. Open Thur–Sun lunch and dinner, Mon dinner only. $$. This friendly café serves good food and some fabulous desserts. BYO.

Byron Bay

The Beach Café

Clark's Beach. Tel: (02) 6685 7598. Open daily breakfast and lunch. $$. Simply the best breakfast and brunch in Byron, on the veranda overlooking the beach.

Byron Thai

31 Lawson St. Tel: (02) 6685 8453. Open daily for dinner. $$. Courteous service, succulent meat and delicious seafood spiced with fragrant herbs and sauces. BYO and licensed.

Fresh

7 Jonson St. Open daily, no bookings. $. Seafood and vegetarian restaurant with shared tables, enormous portions and risible prices. BYO.

Misaki Byron

11 Fletcher St. Tel: (02) 6685 7966. Open Wed–Fri for lunch, Tue–Sat for dinner. $$$. Unusual Japanese dishes on a candlelit covered terrace. BYO.

Raving Prawn

Feros Arcade, Jonson St. Tel: (02) 6685 6737. $$$. Run by Nick, a Geordie turned native. Seafood *par excellence*. BYO.

Coffs Harbour

Fishermen's Co-op

The marina. Tel: (02) 6652 2811. Open Mon–Thur 1030–1830, Fri–Sun 1030–1900. $. Pick your *poisson* from the best of the day's catch – flake, flathead, trawl whiting – and they'll barbecue it, grill it, crumb-coat it or fry it in butter to take away.

Fountain Restaurant

388 High St. Tel: (02) 6651 1978. $. Spicy Vietnamese dishes pepper the menu at this busy restaurant. BYO.

Maria's

368 High St. Tel: (02) 6651 3000. Open Wed–Mon from 1730. $$. Great pizza and pasta plus a range of meat dishes in a welcoming and friendly atmosphere. BYO.

Scoffs

386 High St. Tel: (02) 6651 1516. Open daily for dinner. $$$. The delicious Australian cuisine is distinctly modern, but the turn-of-the-century photos adorning the walls take you back to Coffs Harbour, pre-tourism, 1890–1932. The nearby sister restaurant, Scoffees (*tel: (02) 6651 1544, open Wed–Mon lunch and dinner; $$*) specialises in 'bush' cuisine.

Up the Creek Café

Coffs promenade. Open Tue–Sun 0900–1700. $. Watch the seagulls ducking into the creek over a breakfast of frothy coffee and fresh muffins on the outdoor veranda, snuggled between the bougainvillaea trees.

Grafton

Crown Hotel

Prince St. Tel: (02) 6642 4000. $. Breakfast, lunch and dinner on offer at bargain prices at this colonial hotel. It's no-frills food, but the location is lovely, with tables on an outdoor terrace overlooking the river.

Roches Family Hotel Bistro

85 Victoria St. Tel: (02) 6642 2866. Open Mon–Sat lunch and dinner. $$. The food at this 1870s hotel could easily rival city establishments. Choose from delicacies such as barramundi in rock melon salsa or scallops crumbed in coconut, followed up by a beer and chat at the bar with inquisitive locals.

Nimbin

Choices

Cullen St. Tel: (02) 6689 1698. $$. Serves tasty snacks such as nachos, lamb souvlaki, falafel and great sandwiches to be enjoyed on the outside terrace.

The Rainbow Café

Cullen St. $. Infamous as a dope-smoking joint, it offers a range of burgers and sandwiches, plus freshly squeezed juices. For a true stomach-churning experience, order celery or beetroot juice.

Shopping

Byron Bay is great for shopping with many individual, quirky boutiques. Shops to look out for include **Aspidistra** (*6 Jonson St*) for beautiful handprinted fabrics and clothes, **Tir Nan Og** (*19–23 Lawson St*) for delightful children's gear, and the **Byron Bay Hat Co** (*4 Jonson St*) for the best bush hats around. For the trendiest surf gear, try **Maddog Surf** (*91 Jonson St*). For ceramics, arts and crafts, head to **Bellingen**, which has an exceptional choice of paintings, sculptures pottery, jewellery and more at **The Yellow Shed** (*2 Hyde St*). The **Old Butter Factory** south of the town is a wonderful old wooden building with leather, ceramics, antiques, glass and woodcraft shops and studios. On the main street is the historic **Hammond and Wheatley Emporium**, which offers elegant clothing and, upstairs, the upmarket **Sweetwater** art and craft gallery. **Nimbin's art gallery** (*Cullen St; open daily 1000–1600*) sells a range of beautiful crafts including handpainted furniture, colourful fishy vases, mirrors and sculpture.

Nightlife

Byron Bay undoubtedly has the best nightlife in this area, with some good pubs and lots of live music. Check out the local *Byronshire Echo/Byronshire News* for what's on. Around Coffs Harbour, bands play at the **Coffs Ex-Services Club** (*Vernon St; tel: (02) 6652 3888*) with big names at the **RSL** in Sawtell (*5km south of town; tel: (02) 6653 1577*). In the restaurant complex (*cnr Pacific Highway/Bray St*) the **Greenhouse Tavern** has live music and there's also a large cinema (*tel: (02) 6651 6444*).

Flora and fauna

Much of NSW feels like an exotic garden. Every walk through a national park delivers up yet another colourful bush, every forest a variation on the eucalyptus tree, every shoreline another flower in bloom. The rainforests in particular are a microcosm of diverse life forms – they contain over 80 per cent of the world's plants and animals.

Trees and plants you are most likely to see:

Eucalyptus tree, also known as the gum tree, of which there are over 500 species ranging from the slightly luminous **Sydney blue gum** to the gnarled and twisted **alpine gums**. They're found all over NSW, surviving Australia's harsh climate by storing water and nutrients in their evergreen leaves. Instead, they shed bark and branches, which simply drop off, keeping the ecosystem on track by creating hollows for rosellas, possums and kookaburras.

Strangler Figs have an unusual start in life. After passing through the gut of a hungry bird, the sticky seeds are deposited high up on

FROM COFFS HARBOUR TO BYRON BAY

a tree branch. If the seed germinates, the roots expand downwards, joining together and eventually smothering the host tree. It's commonly found in subtropical rainforests, along with the **yellow carabeen**, which can live up to 800 years and has huge buttress roots, and the **giant stinging tree** – the formic acid emitted through its stinging 'hairs' feels like an ant bite. In coastal and palm rainforests the delightfully named **Blue Lilly Pilly** tree produces a blue cherry-like fruit in summer. **King ferns** and **bird's nest ferns** are common in rainforests as are **walking stick palms**, so called for their long, straight, spindly trunks, and used for that purpose.

Paterson's Curse transforms the landscape into purple meadows in spring and summer, a 'curse' because cattle who over-indulge end up with bloated stomachs. However it's known as Salvation Jane in a drought because it continues to grow well, providing sheep fodder. **Christmas bells** set the countryside ablaze with red and yellow in December and January.

The red **bottlebrush tree**, a member of the 50-plus varieties of the Banksia family, looks just like its name, whilst the perfumed, purple **jacaranda** tree is a beautiful addition to the landscape when it flowers from mid October to mid November.

“ *Rainforests are nature's cathedrals.* ”
Bushranger at Dorrigo National Park

South of Sydney

Quaint villages rooted in the 1830s, the highest mountain in Australia, beaches where kangaroos play in the surf, national parks where parrots and wallabies outnumber the tourists. The area south of Sydney is a wonderfully kept secret, which many visitors miss in their haste to enjoy the treasures of the coast further north. Tourism has been slow to take off here – the long sweeping beaches give the impression of virgin sand, the landscape possesses a wild, untamed beauty and the cooler climate keeps the lush southern highlands a velvety shade of green – visit whilst it's still asleep.

SOUTH OF SYDNEY

BEST OF
South of Sydney

Getting there: **Berrima and Bowral:** *From Sydney, take the M5 Metroad which leads into the South Western Expressway, then into the Hume Highway. Both are a short detour off the highway. There are also several daily trains from Sydney.*

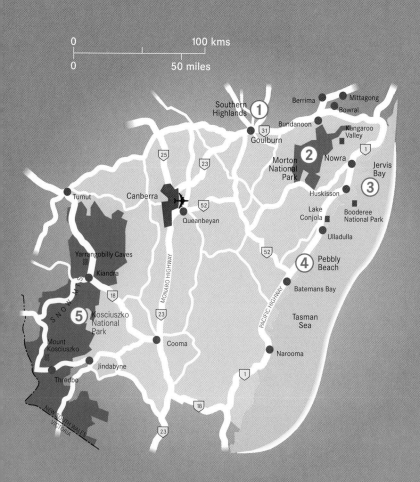

0			100 kms
0		50 miles	

Southern Highlands ①
Berrima
Mittagong
Bowral
Bundanoon
Goulburn
31
Kangaroo Valley
1
Morton National Park ②
Nowra
Jervis Bay
25
23
Tumut
Canberra
52
Huskisson
③
Queanbeyan
Lake Conjola
Booderee National Park
Ulladulla
Yarrangobilly Caves
52
MONARO HIGHWAY
④ Pebbly Beach
Kiandra
18
Batemans Bay
⑤ Kosciuszko National Park
Tasman Sea
Mount Kosciuszko
Cooma
PACIFIC HIGHWAY
23
Jindabyne
Narooma
Thredbo
1
NEW SOUTH WALES
VICTORIA
18
23

① The villages that time forgot

The Southern Highlands are awash with sleepy little villages such as Bundanoon and Berrima, which seem to have sidestepped development, depending on curious tourists and a burgeoning afternoon tea and arts and crafts industry to keep them on the map. They won't set your adrenalin pumping – quite the opposite – but an afternoon browsing through their artistic treasures will make you seriously question the merits of big-city living. **Pages 136–137**

② Morton National Park

Deep in the heart of the Southern Highlands, this is sandstone scenery at its best, peppered with fabulous walks through rainforest gullies, the magnificent Fitzroy Falls and the bizarre Glow Worm Glen, sparkling at night with the blue luminescence emitted from gnats' larvae.
Pages 136–137

③ Jervis Bay

There are few places in New South Wales that are more rewarding to the senses than Jervis Bay. Deserted white sandy beaches with crystal-clear water, beautiful forests, a colourful bird population and a spectacular underwater world make this a relaxing retreat for a peaceful few days. **Page 138**

④ Pebbly Beach

When you're bouncing and bumping down the 7km that lead to this beach (which is sandy, despite its name), you'll be wondering if it's worth it. It is. Not only is the 'bush meets the sea' setting exceptionally picturesque, but the resident kangaroos and colourful birds are far more interesting beach companions than any holiday reading. With a bit of luck, you might even catch a humpback whale on its migratory route. **Page 140**

⑤ Kosciuszko National Park

Australia's semi-arid landscape possesses only 250 square kilometres of alpine land and half of those lie in NSW on the section of the Great Dividing Range north of Mount Kosciuszko. Named after a Polish general by Paul Strzelecki, who climbed the mountain in 1840, Kosciuszko offers Australia's best skiing in winter and hearty, bracing mountain air and activities in summer.
Pages 140–141

135

Tourist information

Cooma Visitor's Centre: *119 Sharp St, Cooma. Tel: (02) 6450 1742/toll free 1800 636 525.*
Berrima Courthouse and information centre: *cnr Wilshire and Argyle Sts. Tel: (02) 4877 1505.*
Booderee National Park Visitor Centre, Jervis Bay: *Tel: (02) 4443 0977.*
Fitzroy Falls Visitor's Centre, Fitzroy Falls: *Tel: (02) 4887 7270.*
Shoalhaven Visitor's Centre: *Princes Highway, Ulladulla. Tel: (02) 4455 1269.*

The Southern Highlands

Berrima

A quaint 1830s' village that time forgot, Berrima invites leisurely lunches and afternoons browsing in the many craft and antique shops. Originally intended as the manufacturing

centre of the region owing to its good water supply and fertile soil, an imposing sandstone courthouse and gaol were built in 1838. However, it was bypassed by the railway and the grand plans – and population – dwindled away. Today the courthouse is a museum (*Wilshire St; open daily 1000–1600; $$*), much of which is devoted to a re-creation of the famous trial of two immigrant convicts, **Lucretia Dunkley** and her lover, **Martin Beech**, who were hanged in 1843 for murdering Lucretia's husband. There's also an interesting room that shows the parallel history of the world, Australia and Berrima throughout the 1900s.

Bowral

Nowhere near as quaint as Berrima, Bowral has two main claims to fame. One is the spectacular **Tulip Time Festival** at the beginning of October in Corbett Gardens (*Wingecarribee St*). The other is the **Bradman Museum** (*St Jude St; tel: (02) 4862 1247; open daily 1000–1600; $$*), a shrine to Australia's most famous cricketer, Sir Donald Bradman, who began his career on the Bowral Oval in the 1920s. It traces the history of Australian and international cricket from the first match played in Sydney in 1804 to the present day, with an upstairs section dedicated solely to Bradman's life. Cricket aficionados will love it and even those who don't know a wicket from a leg before might muster some enthusiasm.

Bundanoon and Morton National Park

A top destination for honeymooners in the 1940s, when newly-weds packed out more than 50 guesthouses, Bundanoon, 'a place of deep gullies', has slipped into a slumber since then. It's now a picturesque olde worlde village that makes an excellent base for exploring Morton National Park.

The Brigadoon festival

The Southern Highlands were popular with early settlers because of the cooler climate and four distinct seasons, which reminded them of Europe. Bundanoon and nearby Sutton Forest have large immigrant Scottish populations, celebrated in Bundanoon on a Saturday in April by the Brigadoon festival, a tartan spectacle of Scottish dancing, caber tossing and haggis hurling.

Walks in Morton National Park

From Bundanoon, a steep 20-minute walk into the valley at the bottom of William St takes you to **Glow Worm Glen**. On a good day, glow worms cling to the rock face like little luminous clocks lighting up the darkness. You'll need a torch for the walk down but switch it off at the bottom – curious torch beams are killing them off.

One kilometre from Bundanoon is the entrance to the park. Interesting walks include the **Eris Coal Mine** trail across the top of waterfalls, down to a disused coal mine, with plenty of wildflowers such as boronia and honey flowers (Sept–Dec) to admire along the way. The **Fairy Bower** trail, which follows a waterfall down into the valley, really does feel like a stroll through a magical glade along a path lined with king ferns. Bird life, particularly crimson and eastern rosellas, is plentiful.

On the eastern side of Morton, the spectacular **Fitzroy Falls** (*Nowra Rd*) plunge 81m into the Yarrunga Valley. The **West Rim** walk offers heart-stopping panoramas over the sandstone gorge, leading across the top of another gushing cascade, the **Twin Falls**, against a backdrop of yellow-tailed black cockatoos, eastern yellow robins and crimson rosellas dancing above the black wattle and peppermint gum forest.

Kangaroo Valley

From Fitzroy Falls, it's worth a 15km meander down into Kangaroo Valley. Not for the animals, which hide well away from the tourists, but for the glorious drive through lush ferns and gum forest down Barrengarry Mountain. There are several cottage craft and teashops, a pioneer farm museum (*Moss Vale Rd; tel: (02) 4465 1733; open daily 0930–1630; $*) and the impressive 1897 Hampden Bridge over Kangaroo River.

The south coast

The first real point of interest on the south coast is **Jervis Bay**, although the little town of **Kiama**, 120km south of Sydney, is a convenient stopping-off point – its claim to fame is a big and little blowhole which the sea comes whooshing through. Otherwise **Seven Mile Beach**, south of Gerringong, is a great place for a picnic, the long sweep of golden sand disturbed only by a few dog walkers and schoolboy surfers. From there, an attractive drive with ocean views and green hills leads to Jervis Bay, which was first sighted in 1770 by Captain Cook and finally named in 1791 after Rear-Admiral Sir John Jervis. Today it is famed for its clean waters and dazzling white sands, an idyllic spot of untouched paradise.

Booderee National Park

Jervis Bay Road. $$.

Previously earmarked as a site for a nuclear power station, Booderee National Park is now a marine park and nature reserve (with campsites), second only to the Great Barrier Reef for marine diversity. The beaches are spectacular –

Hyams Beach, surrounded by sandstone cliffs, bills itself as having the whitest sand in the world. If you're looking for seclusion, head to **Scottish Rocks**, which sits at the base of a thick patch of forest, where your only companion is likely to be an occasional fisherman. **Green Patch** beach is a favourite fishing and snorkelling spot, perfect for families and abundant with wildlife. The lorikeets, rosellas and kangaroos are very tame and will beg for your sandwiches (but feeding them is harmful). **Murrays Beach** is one of the most picturesque – a long sweep of golden sand, fringed by thick forest and deep sapphire water with a view over Bowen

Island. After the beach, a track off to the left leads through eucalyptus trees to **Governor's Head**, a big flat rock perched on the cliff edge, with dramatic views of the sea swelling past Bowen Island and crashing onto the rocks. The ruined **Cape St George Lighthouse** (down the very rough Stony Creek Rd) offers a stunning panorama over Wreck Bay, so called because of the many shipwrecks which occurred there in the 19th century.

Within the park, **Jervis Bay Botanic Gardens** (*Cave Beach Rd; open weekdays 0800–1600, Sat Christmas– Easter, and Sun 1000–1700; admission included in park fee*) are perfect for shady walks in the rainforest gully, amongst the orchids, rhododendrons and bottlebrushes.

Huskisson

Signposted off Princes Highway, South of Nowra.

This tiny town is the closest you'll find to a commercial centre. Activities on offer include the extremely popular **dolphin watch tours** (*$$*) (*Dolphin Watch, 50 Owen St; tel: (02) 4441 6311 – booking advisable*), **game fishing** (*$$$*) and **reel fishing** (*$*) (*Jervis Bay Tackle Co; 57 Owen St; tel: (02) 4441 6377*). **Snorkelling** (*$$*) and **scuba diving** (*$$$*) are very pleasurable in Jervis Bay's sheltered, temperate waters, which deliver up rewards such as huge cuttlefish, weedy sea dragons, corals and Port Jackson sharks (*Pro Dive, 64 Owen St; tel: (02) 4441 5255*).

Lady Denman Heritage Complex

Dent St, Huskisson.

Enjoy a peaceful boardwalk through the mangrove swamps amongst the sea eagles or spend a while browsing in the **Lady Denman Maritime Museum** (*open Tue–Fri 1300–1600, weekends 1000–1600; $$*). It houses a fascinating display about the aborigines, the original inhabitants of Jervis Bay, and includes items used for shelter, fishing and hunting. There's also a section on diving (including a suit from 1914), whaling and shipwrecks, as well as a collection of old barometers, compasses, seaman's boxes and ornate ships' figureheads to delight old sea dogs.

Lake Conjola

North of Ulladulla.

Edged with lush green forest, the beautiful Lake Conjola is popular with families and fishermen. There's a public reserve at the end of the caravan park, with sandy beaches and a proliferation of king parrots and galahs.

Pebbly Beach

Take the turning to Depot Beach off the Princes Highway.

Halfway between the pretty little harbourside town of Ulladulla and Bateman's Bay lies Pebbly Beach, a wild, sandy beach sandwiched between sandstone cliffs and thick forest. Its main attraction is the large kangaroo population that lives around the campsite by the beach, and can sometimes be spotted playing in the waves, along with crimson rosellas and galahs.

Kosciuszko National Park and the Snowy Mountains

From Canberra, take the Manaro Highway to Cooma. Turn left off route 18 a few kilometres west of town, following signs to Thredbo via Benidale and Jindabyne. $$$ per day.

Situated on the southeast border between NSW and Victoria, Kosciuszko is the state's largest national park. It contains NSW's only ski fields and half of the country's snow area, including Australia's highest mountain, Mount Kosciuszko at 2228m.

Thredbo

Thredbo's wooden chalets nestle amongst the snow gums in an alpine valley. In winter it's packed with skiers from all over the state. It markets itself as an all-year-round resort, with a wide-ranging summer activities programme. All activities can be booked through the **Thredbo Centre** (*tel: (02) 6459 4100*) at the bottom of the ski lift. Nearby **Raw NRG Thredbo** (*tel: (02) 6457 6282*) runs mountain bike courses and rents equipment.

Many people come to Thredbo to climb to the 'top of Australia', **Mount Kosciuszko**, an easy 6.5km walk (one way) over a raised metal walkway from the top of the **Crackenback chairlift** (*from Thredbo centre; $$*), which runs all year round. Further down, other beautiful walks include the 3.2km Meadows Nature Track, which leads through alpine gums along the river.

Yarrangobilly Caves

Snowy Mountains Highway. Open daily 0900–1630. $$.

If you're not pushed for time, a detour to Yarrangobilly will give you a sense of Australia's vastness. After Kiandra, the terrain becomes almost lunar-like, dotted with eerily twisted snow gums. There are six caves at Yarrangobilly. The largest is called the **Glory Hole**, less than 100,000 years old, which you can explore on your own. Of the others, the **Jillebenan** (*tours at 1100/1500*) and the **Jersey** (*tours at 1300*) are the most decorative. At the bottom of the valley is a glorious thermal pool surrounded by snow gums – a scenic setting for a (nearly) warm swim all year round.

Restaurants

The Southern Highlands

Berrima

Berrima Bakery

Wingecarribee St. $$. Pick up a picnic of tomato bread, pumpkin damper or leek pie, as well as some delightful cakes. There's also a little coffee shop to the side.

The Surveyor General Inn

Old Hume Highway. Tel: (02) 4877 1226. Open daily lunch and dinner. $$. Opened in 1835, this is the oldest continuously licensed hotel in Australia, serving plenty of ale as well as traditional barbecue food and roasts.

White Horse Inn

Market Place. Tel: (02) 4877 1204. Open daily 0800–2100. $$$. Sophisticated food in the elegant historic surroundings of this 1832 inn.

Bundanoon

The Post Office Café

27 Railway Ave. Tel: (02) 4883 6354. Open Wed–Sun for lunch, Wed–Sat for dinner. $$. The service can be snail-like, but the innovative modern Australian dishes are excellent, served in pretty plant-filled surroundings.

Ye Olde Bicycle Shoppe Tearoom

9 Church St. Tel: (02) 4883 6043. Open 1000–1700, Thur–Mon, more often in summer. $$. Classical music plays lightly in the background, early 1900s' bikes hang on the walls and the cakes are second to none. You can also hire bikes here.

Kangaroo Valley

Hampden Bridge Tearooms

Moss Vale Rd. Open daily 0900–1700. $$. The terrace at the back has wonderful views over the bridge and river – perfect for a Devonshire tea or lunchtime snack.

South Coast

Huskisson, Jervis Bay

The Husky Pub (*open 1000–2300, midnight at weekends; $$*) serves no-frills bar food of burgers and steaks, in a traditional pub atmosphere complete with pool tables, live bands on a Friday and roaring log fires in winter.

Ulladulla

Good seafood restaurants here include the upmarket **Tory's** (*30 Wason St; tel: (02) 4454 0888; open Sun lunch and daily for dinner; $$$*) with a take-away downstairs, and the **Harbourside** (*84 Princes Highway; tel: (02) 4455 3377; open daily lunch and dinner; $$*), which has an outdoor terrace with lovely views.

Snowy Mountains

Thredbo

Café Avalanche

At the bottom of the ski lift. $. Simply the best raspberry muffins in the southern hemisphere.

Reds

Squatters Run. Tel: (02) 6457 6083. Open daily lunch and dinner. $$. Under the watchful gaze of a stag's head, fragrant dishes such as marinated chicken with peanut and coriander pesto are served with a smile.

T-Bar

Mowamba Mall. Tel: (02) 6457 6355. Open daily from 1800. $$. This fully licensed restaurant serves chargrilled steaks and seafood in cosy surroundings. Children's menu available.

The **Alpine Hotel** encompasses a variety of restaurants ranging from the upmarket **Cascades** (*open breakfast, lunch (winter only) and dinner; $$–$$$*) to the self-service **Bistro** (*open all year 1000–2400; $*). Après-skiers head to the **Schuss Bar** which has live music (*1600–1930 Mon–Sat, open weekends in summer; $$*), followed by the **Keller Bar**, which parties until 0300 (*closed in summer; $$*).

Shopping

Bundanoon

Bundanoon Art Gallery (*cnr Railway Ave and William St; open daily 1000–1600*) has unusual handmade jewellery, mosaics, glassware, sculpture and paintings within every price range. **Bundanoon Memorial Hall** (*Railway Ave*) hosts a country fair on the first Sunday of each month – a mixture of bric-à-brac, homemade cooking and crafts (*open 0900–1500*).

Berrima

There's a myriad of art and craft shops lining the main street, the Old Hume Highway. Shops worth looking out for include the **Berrima Bear Company** for teddy bears, **Past Times** for olde worlde curios and art supplies, **Berrima Galleries** for upmarket watercolours, jewellery, ceramics and glass and the **Little Hand-stirred Jam Shop**, a gourmet's delight of unusual marinades, sauces and pickles as well as way-out jams and honey.

What to buy

For genuine indigenous artefacts – jacaranda seed-pod jewellery, engraved emu eggs, clapsticks – drop into **Timberrys Aboriginal Arts and Crafts** (*Lady Denman Heritage Complex, Dent St, Huskisson; open daily 1000–1600*). The owner, Laddie, is a real showman, offering didgeridoo and boomerang demonstrations, and explanations of aboriginal decorative symbols.

143

The Aborigines

When the First Fleet landed in Sydney in 1788, there were probably around 300,000 aborigines living in the whole of Australia. They lived in small, scattered groups, mainly along the coast where the sea provided a rich source of food and the rainfall was higher.

Jervis Bay was home to several such groups, described by **Governor Macquarie** in 1811 as 'well made good looking men, perfectly at their ease and void of fear'. Like many

indigenous tribes in the early days of European settlement, they acted as guides, in this case to the impenetrable bushland. They did not realise that the white settlers would dispossess them of their land, claiming *terra nullius* – that the territory belonged to no one. As land is the very core of aboriginal ancestral origins and culture, the aborigines could not have suffered a worse fate, likened by **Robert Hughes** in *The Fatal Shore* to condemning them to 'spiritual death'.

All over NSW, the introduction of sheep and cattle drove out

> I could tell you of heartbreak, hatred blind,
> I could tell of crimes that shame mankind,
> Brutal wrong and deeds malign,
> Of rape and murder, son of mine.
> But I'll tell instead of brave and fine,
> When lives of black and white entwine,
> And men in brotherhood combine,
> This would I tell you, son of mine. "

Son of Mine, 1964, by Aboriginal poet Oodgeroo Noonuccal

the kangaroos and native game causing the breakdown of the hunting environment. European diseases such as smallpox, influenza and measles wiped out large numbers. Violent clashes with the settlers and the introduction of alcohol killed many more. Within 100 years of settlement, total numbers had declined to around 50,000.

Throughout the 19th and 20th centuries, the aborigines were subjected to discrimination at all levels and omitted from the population census until the 1960s. Many children were taken from their parents and placed with white families to learn to think and act 'white' under the government's policy of assimilation.

However, by the 1970s, aboriginal issues were creeping onto the political agenda. A land rights movement gathered momentum, publicised by the **Aboriginal Tent Embassy** (*see page 156*) outside Canberra's Parliament House. Several steps have been taken to hand land back to indigenous tribes as part of a reconciliation process, particularly in the Northern Territories. On the south coast, Jervis Bay's national park was transferred to the aboriginal community in 1995 and renamed **Booderee**, 'plenty of fish'. However, great inequality remains. Indigenous people have a higher infant mortality rate and poorer housing, sanitation and food supplies than other Australians. On the positive side a strong aboriginal culture of writers, dancers and artists has emerged, receiving widespread recognition.

145

> I thought that's a real indictment upon Australia that Aboriginal people living in an advanced country have third world health problems. "

Dr Sandra Eades, Aboriginal Medical Service, in *My Kind Of People: Achievement Identity and Aboriginality*, 1994

CANBERRA

Canberra

Much maligned by other Australians, who curse 'Canberra', when they really mean the federal government, this ultra-modern city has received some fierce criticism. It's definitely a place that you'll either love or hate, but its plus points are many. Planned as a city within a garden, there's lots of lush green space, a backdrop of mountains and thousands of trees – which other capital city has kangaroos bouncing about just a stone's throw from its Houses of Parliament? But that's not all. The excellent restaurants (minus the Sydney prices) will keep foodies happy, whilst culture buffs can soak up the magnificent art gallery and impressive museums.

BEST OF
Canberra

Getting around: Canberra is too big to visit on foot, although it's easy to drive around and most of the major tourist attractions have large, free car parks. The **Canberra Explorer Bus** *(tel: 132 251) does a 2-hour tour of the city, or you can purchase a pass ranging from four hours to three days, which allows you to hop on, hop off. Bus 901 covers the main sights south of the lake and northeast, whilst bus 904 encompasses the northwest. Buses depart from platform 11, City Bus Interchange, East Row (tel: 131 710). Bicycles are an ideal way to visit the city (see* **Mr Spokes** *page 152).*

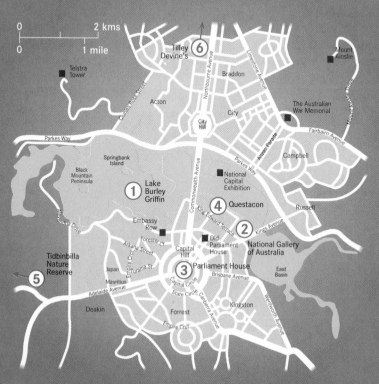

① On your bike

Canberra was built just after the invention of the motor car, so its roads are wide and straight, making it one of the easiest cities to drive around in Australia. But the real glory of Canberra is that it has over 300km of cycleways. Thirty-three of those encircle the beautiful Lake Burley Griffin, with every turn of the pedal taking you past flower-filled parks and right into the National Gallery's sculpture garden. **Page 152**

② National Gallery of Australia

The architect of the National Gallery of Australia, Colin Madigan, said: 'In my opinion, a gallery is supposed to act like a cathedral to lift the spirits of the people.' And that's exactly what this spacious gallery does. From Australian impressionism to international masterpieces and aboriginal bark paintings, each room has its own charm. But perhaps the true gem is the lakeside sculpture garden – art, air and the lunchtime chimes of the 53-bell Carillon. **Pages 154–155**

③ Parliament House

Described by writer Mark Lawson as having 'all the original Aussie brio of the Sydney Opera House', Parliament House stands majestically at the southern tip of the Parliamentary Triangle, formed by Capital Hill, Commonwealth and Kings Avenues. Burrowed so far into the side of the hill you can walk over its roof, the architecture alone is reason enough to visit, although a glimpse of parliamentary question time is comforting proof that politicians are the same everywhere. **Pages 156–157**

④ Questacon Science and Technology Centre

There's an earthquake in one corner, a tornado in another . . . this bright, vibrant science museum has so many buttons to press, experiments to watch, handles to pull, that you find yourself wanting to join the kids in rushing helter-skelter down the spiral walkway to be the first to freeze your shadow on the wall. **Page 158**

⑤ Walk with the animals

Tidbinbilla Nature Reserve offers the chance to see as much wildlife as you'd see in a zoo, but roaming free in its natural habitat. Kangaroos, emus and exotic birds abound, whilst a few loose enclosures give endangered species such as koalas and rock wallabies a fighting chance. **Page 159**

⑥ Tune into the vibes

Canberra has a younger-than-average population, which means a better-than-average music scene, and where better to start than the intimate atmosphere of Tilley Devine's? The dark wooded booths and sumptuous fabrics are reminiscent of a 1940s' cabaret club, where you can linger over a coffee, indulge in dinner or linger over a bottle of wine. Several nights a week, the stage lights up with student jazz musicians, local rock bands, big name groups or poetry readings. **Page 161**

Tourist information

Canberra Visitors Centre: *330 Northbourne Ave, Dickson. Tel: (02) 6205 0044/1800 026 166 www.canberratourism.com.au. Open 0900–1800.*
Tidbinbilla Visitor Centre: *Tidbinbilla Nature Reserve. Open Mon–Fri 0900– 1630, weekends 0900–1730. $$.*

149

Canberra: an introduction

A visit to Canberra prompted travel journalist, Jan Morris, to write: 'I miss the social and aesthetic density that is the profoundest purpose of a city – the intimate association of people of all kinds, inhabiting every kind of building, jammed together in din and bustle and misery and joy.'

Indeed, with its modern buildings and symmetrical road system, Canberra is highly unusual, not least because it was purpose built from nothing on sheep-grazing land and planned from the outset.

When the six colonies of Australia united in a federation in 1901, the country needed somewhere to house the government. Both Sydney and Melbourne staked their claim, and, unable to agree, the site of Canberra, within its own tiny state, the **Australian Capital Territory** (ACT), was eventually chosen as a compromise, halfway between the two.

An international design competition was held, and the plans of an American architect, **Walter Burley Griffin**, were selected. His vision was to create a symbolic and symmetrical city centred around a man-made lake, in harmony with the surrounding landscape. When work began in 1913, the city was built out rather than up, resulting in a bright, airy capital, stretching 35km, north to south. All properties are on a 99-year lease so that the government retains tight control over the city's development.

For many years the city remained practically empty of people, with just 5000 inhabitants after World War II. Today, there are around 300,000, with the vast majority employed in government offices. However, if the moves currently afoot to build an international airport at Canberra to rival Sydney's go to plan, this spacious city could find itself nearly half full.

The Australian War Memorial

Limestone Ave, Campbell. Tel: (02) 6243 4261. Bus 901 and Canberra Explorer. Open daily 1000–1700, but an extensive redevelopment programme means that some museum exhibitions may be closed. A bugle plays the last post at closing time. Guided tours roughly every hour 1000–1400. Free.

Part memorial, part museum, this tribute to the Australians who have died in wars this century is a moving one. Standing at the top of the monument-lined Anzac parade, where the red gravel signifies blood shed, the tranquil walls surrounding the **Pool of Reflection** are engraved with the 102,000 names of Australia's war dead. **The Tomb of the Unknown Soldier**, one of 46,000 Australians who died on the Western Front in World War I, lies in the domed **Hall of Memory**. This peaceful building contains one of the world's largest mosaics, made from 6 million Italian tiles and painstakingly assembled by war widows (*under restoration until 2001, but still accessible*).

Downstairs is an impressive military museum, with excellent exhibitions spanning the many wars in which Australia has participated, from the Korean War and Vietnam to the World Wars and the Gulf War. Displays include uniforms, weapons, mementoes and re-creations of the battles, as well as rocket launchers, armoured personnel carriers, and helicopters. The World War II gallery, reopened in 1999 after a $20 million redevelopment, is particularly moving, brought alive by personal testimonies, love letters and diaries alongside the military memorabilia. The Bradbury aircraft hall (scheduled to reopen in May 2000 but much of the collection is still on display, interspersed around the other galleries) includes

the Lancaster Bomber 'G' for George, which serves as a reminder of the 4000 Australians who died while flying with the RAF bomber command during World War II.

Embassy Row

Canberra Explorer and bus 901.

If you're feeling patriotic, head down to Yarralumla, the diplomatic precinct, where all the embassies and high commissions are based. Buildings range from the beautifully ornate and culturally distinctive (Thailand, Papua New Guinea, India) to the dull and dreary (Poland, Finland).

Lake Burley Griffin

Bus 901 to National Capital Exhibition Commonwealth Park or the National Gallery leaves you on the lakeshore.

A city built around a lake was central to Walter Burley Griffin's original plan, although this only came to fruition in 1963, when the Molonglo River was dammed. Situated between the triangle of Black Mountain, Capital Hill and Mount Ainslie, the lake's landmarks include the **Captain Cook Memorial Jet**, which spurts 147m high (*operates daily 1000–1200, 1400–1600*), and the **Carillon** bells, a jubilee present from Britain in 1963, which ring out classical tunes along with the occasional Pink Panther theme. For a closer look, head to **Lake Burley Griffin Boat Hire** (*Ferry Terminal, Barrine Drive*) and explore in a canoe, paddle boat or aqua bike (*$$*). Near by is **Mr Spokes** bike and rollerblade hire (*open Wed–Sun 0900–1700, daily during school holidays*). A cycleway runs right round the lake, so it's perfect for exploring by bike.

National Capital Exhibition

Regatta Point, Commonwealth Park. Open 0900–1700 (until 1800 in summer). Bus 901 and Canberra Explorer. Free.

For an effortless understanding of Canberra's history, head to the National Capital Exhibition on the banks of the lake. Here, laser displays, short audio-visual shows and old photographs unravel the story behind this manicured city.

Mount Ainslie and Telstra Tower

Both the Canberra Explorer and bus 904 go to the Telstra Tower.

Walter Burley Griffin planned Canberra around the Capital Hill–Mount Ainslie axis. At 843m high, Mount Ainslie is one of the best vantage points over the city (particularly at sunset), with views over the lake, Anzac parade, the House of Parliament, and the foothills of the Snowy Mountains in the distance. You can drive up, or hike up the pretty trail from behind the War Memorial, where you may bounce into kangaroos which live at the base of the mountain. The 195m-tall Telstra communications tower on **Black Mountain** (*open daily 0900–2200; $*) to the west also offers a splendid panorama, as well as a revolving restaurant.

Parliamentary apologies

In June 1997, Bob Carr, the Premier of New South Wales, made a significant step towards recognising the injustices meted out to the indigenous people. He called upon the Parliament of New South Wales to apologise for its part in enacting the laws and policies that resulted in the separation of children from their families. The resolution was passed unanimously.

153

The National Gallery of Australia

Parkes Place. Open daily 1000–1700. Free guided tours of Australian and International sections, daily, 1100 and 1400. Tours of the aboriginal section, Thur and Sun 1100. Self-guided audio tours are available. Bus 901 and Canberra Explorer. Free.

This spacious and uncluttered art gallery is a pleasure to visit. The core of the collection is Australian, with a large selection of indigenous art. The strength of the international collection lies in contemporary paintings with a few important pre-1800 European works, whilst the beautiful lakeside gardens house a wonderful variety of sculptures.

The Australian collection

Highlights include several impressionistic paintings from the Heidelberg School (*see pages 24–25*) such as *Golden Summer, Eaglemont* (1889) by **Arthur Streeton** and **Tom Roberts**'s beautiful bushland painting *In a corner on the Macintyre* (1895). *Weighing the Fleece* (1921), by **George W Lambert**, is one of the best-known pictures in Australian art, reflecting the prosperity of the farmers after World War I. An important contribution to post-war art is the *Ned Kelly series* (1945–7) by **Sidney Nolan**. It explores ideas about authority and violence in the direct aftermath of World War II. **Fred Williams**, one of Australia's artistic stars in the 1960s, portrayed the countryside as a vast abstract space, as seen in his *Lysterfield triptych* (1967–8).

Aboriginal art

Aboriginal people depend heavily on pictures, dance and oral tradition to pass their culture down the generations, as they have no written language to record their knowledge.

Highlights include the traditional eucalyptus-bark painting, the *Wagilag Creation Story* (1963) by **Dawidi**, depicting social rules, whilst **Mick Namarari Tjapaltjarri**'s *Sunrise Chasing Away the Night* (1977–8) shows the recent trend of using acrylic paints in indigenous art. **Robert Campbell**'s series of paintings use a combination of the traditional dot technique and human figures. The poignant *Aboriginal Memorial* (1987–8) features 200 hollow log coffins, traditionally used in burial ceremonies. Each one marks a year of European settlement and commemorates the thousands of aboriginals who have died defending their land.

International art

The 20th-century contributions form the bulk of the collection, but important 18th-century works include **Giambattista Tiepolo**'s *Marriage Allegory* (1750), originally designed as a ceiling panel. **Jackson Pollock**'s *Blue Poles* (1952) is probably the most famous painting in the gallery, but also look out for **Willem de Kooning**'s *Woman V* (1952–3), **Pablo Picasso**'s *Luncheon on the Grass*, **Andy Warhol**'s *Elvis* and the huge *Trapeze artists* by **Fernand Léger**.

Sculpture garden

Joggers pass through, old men play boules, schoolchildren sketch here . . . and in amongst the beautiful trees and shrubs, this lakeside garden is home to contemporary and classical sculpture including **Bert Flugelman**'s mirror-surfaced *Cones* (1976–82) and *La Montagne* (1937) by **Aristide Maillol**.

Move with the times

In the 1970s, modern paints and canvas were introduced to an isolated aboriginal area in Papunya, Alice Springs, which became the birthplace of aboriginal art on canvas. Until that time, art had mainly been restricted to body art or carvings on the ground. The traditional bark paintings did not serve a decorative purpose but were designed to instruct people through a story.

Old Parliament House

King George Terrace, Parkes. Tel: (02) 6270 8222. Open daily 0900–1600. $.
Bus 901 and Canberra Explorer.

Intended as a 'temporary solution', this grand building housed
the government for over 60 years until 1988, when the (new)

Parliament House was opened.
It's now home to the **National
Portrait Gallery**, which exalts
Australia's good and great,
from sportsmen (Donald
Bradman) to singers (Kylie
Minogue), explorers, scientists
and businessmen. There's
also a light and sound show,
'Order, Order' in the **House
of Representatives**, which
maps out some of the defining
moments in the building's history.

Situated on the lawns outside is the **aboriginal tent embassy**.
It was first established on Australia Day in 1972 and has
remained there on and off for over 30 years providing a focus
for aboriginal campaigns for land rights and social justice.
It was called an embassy to symbolise the feeling of many
indigenous people that they were essentially foreigners in
their own country.

Parliament House

Capital Hill. Open daily 0900–1700. Recorded infoline: (02) 6277 2727.
Free tours run every half-hour. Canberra Explorer and bus 901.

Burley Griffin's desire to create a city within a garden, blending
buildings into the landscape, is stylishly executed with the
new Parliament House. The government's new home was
dug into the side of a hill and landscaped over the top, with
90 per cent of the building underground. You can walk
over the roof – Australians say it's a symbolic reminder that
democracy can't be stamped upon. Indeed, it's a real people's
palace, where the public can wander in and out at will, admire
the huge contemporary art collection or watch parliamentary
proceedings from the public gallery.

At a cost of over 1 billion dollars, the décor, stonework and wooden marquetry panelling are exquisite. Ninety per cent of the materials used were Australian, although the white marble of the veranda is from Carrara, Italy. Inside, the foyer's 48 green-grey marble pillars represent the eucalyptus forests of Australia, whilst water flowing over a slab of granite muffles the sound of ministers' voices in the central **Member's Hall**, keeping their secrets safe.

You can visit the **House of Representatives**, the **Senate**, and the **Great Hall**, where a 20m tapestry of a eucalyptus forest hangs, based on a painting by **Arthur Boyd**. It took 13 weavers two and a half years to complete, weaving in one small extra detail – a white teardrop representing Haley's Comet, which passed over Australia in 1986.

What does it mean?

Symbolism is rife at Parliament House. The aboriginal mosaic in front of the entrance depicts a meeting place, and represents Australia's indigenous heritage. The ceremonial pool is the sea flowing around Australia, the red gravel the country's deserts. Over the door, the coat of arms with the emu and kangaroo bears a special significance – neither animal can walk backwards, said to represent Australia's progressive society.

The **outside** is also impressive with curved granite walls topped by a giant flagmast, the tallest four-legged structure in the world at 81m.

Question time is 1400–1500 when parliament is sitting; arrive very early for a chance to watch ministers at loggerheads or better still, book (*tel: (02) 6277 4899*).

157

Questacon

The National Science and Technology Centre, King Edward Terrace. 24-hour recorded infoline: 1800 020 603. Open daily 1000–1700. $$. Bus 901 and Canberra Explorer.

A hi-tech spiral walkway leads through fascinating galleries brimming with temporary and permanent interactive exhibits and do-it-yourself experiments. Of the permanent galleries, one is devoted to force, where you can see 3 million volts of electricity crackling in a lightning display, rattle about on an earthquake simulator and understand how a hovercraft is propelled. Another gallery is devoted to light and sound, with appearance-altering mirrors, a delayed speech monitor, a bionic ear, and best of all, a frozen shadow section, where you assume a silly pose, wait for the light to flash, then move away, leaving the shadow frozen to the wall. Education has never been such fun.

Tidbinbilla Nature Reserve

Tel: (02) 6205 1233. Open 0900–1800. Visitor centre open Mon–Fri 1000–1600; Sat–Sun 0900–1630. $$ per car. 45km southwest of Canberra, via Paddy's River Rd.

This 5500-hectare nature reserve offers the perfect opportunity to see native Australian animals in a semi-wild environment. Emus and eastern grey kangaroos roam the surrounding hills, whilst a naturalistic enclosure is home to a band of red

Surrealism

For a truly surreal experience, take a seat in the National Gallery's sculpture garden (see page 155 *) between midday and 1400, when Fujiko Nakaya's* Fog Sculpture *(1976) is in action. A fine water vapour is pumped out over a reed pond, creating an eerie swirling mist even on the hottest days. If you time your visit right, you'll also be able to hear a Carillon bell recital echoing out over the water (* weekdays 1245–1330, weekends 1445–1530; 1245–1330 Wed and weekends in winter *).*

kangaroos. You might also glimpse one of the few hundred rock wallabies left in the world, or a wombat emerging from underground tunnels. There's also a koala breeding area, where around 10–15 koalas are housed at any one time, gradually being released into the wild as numbers grow. They're difficult to see as they blend in so well with the gum trees, but rangers post an up-date of where they are hiding out every morning.

There's also copious bird life at Tidbinbilla with ample opportunity to see kookaburras, galahs and the splendid red-crested gang-gang cockatoo. To ensure a good close-up, the rangers feed the birds at 1430.

Guided tour

Positively the best way to enjoy Tidbinbilla is with friendly native Canberran Sue White. Much wildlife slips past unnoticed, but if there are rock wallabies, echidnas or duck-billed platypus on the move, she'll spot them for you. The day tour also includes a picnic, sampling of 'bush tucker' foods and a dip in a swimming hole at Cotter Dam. Tours run three times a week (*tel: (02) 6259 5999; $$$*).

Restaurants and cafés

Perhaps it's the proliferation of fat-cat politicians with large expense accounts or Canberra's young affluent population that explains why the city is blessed with a huge number of wide-ranging restaurants. Top of the list are the smart, fashionable suburb of Manuka, and Garema Place in the city centre.

Antigo

Petrie Plaza. Tel: (02) 6249 8080. Open daily all day and dinner. $$. An outdoor terrace under the trees, laid-back blues music, and a menu peppered with cajun spices, slow-roasted tomatoes and delicacies such as kangaroo fillets. There's live jazz every Friday 2130–2330: book for this and Saturday nights.

Lemon Grass Thai

71 London Circuit. Tel: (02) 6247 2779. Open Mon–Fri for lunch, Mon–Sat for dinner. $$. This polite, family-friendly restaurant serves a spicy selection of dishes with plenty of choice for vegetarians.

Red Back Café

15 Garema Place. Tel: (02) 6247 1236. Open daily 0900–1030. $$. The modern Australian cuisine encompasses all the specialities – emu, crocodile and kangaroo – plus a fine selection of gourmet sandwiches.

La Scala

Centre Cinema Building. Tel: (02) 6248 8338. Open Mon–Fri for lunch, daily for dinner. $$$. Excellent traditional and contemporary Italian food in upmarket surroundings, great for cosy couple dinners.

Manuka

My Café

Franklin St. Tel: (02) 6295 6632. Open daily till late. $$. This relaxed arty café incorporates native bush foods into the menu in the guise of mint, hazelnut and macadamia pesto and lemon myrtle sauce, concentrating on low fat, low cholesterol – but still tasty – nosh. BYO.

The Ottoman

Franklin St. Tel: (02) 6239 6754. Open Mon–Fri for lunch, Mon–Sat for dinner. $$$. Positively dripping with restaurant awards from the food police, this is Turkish cuisine at its best, served in an opulent, atmospheric dining-room hung with kelims.

Timmy's Kitchen

Furneaux St. Tel: (02) 6295 6537. Open daily for lunch and dinner. $. Small and serviceable, what this restaurant lacks in glamour is made up for by the delicious Chinese and Malaysian food. BYO.

The Tryst

Bougainville St. Tel: (02) 6239 4422. Open daily 1800–2230. $$$. Buzzing with the affluent young and old, this is sophisticated food with an oriental twist.

What to try

If you've seen one Monet too many, head for the **Mirrabook** restaurant in the sculpture garden (*open daily, tel: (02) 6273 2836; $$$*) for lunch on the terrace by the *Fog Sculpture* – it's not just the excellent wine making the delicate dishes of slow-roasted duck and Atlantic salmon appear a little hazy.

Shopping

The huge **Canberra Centre** in the city houses the major department stores, David Jones and Grace Bros, as well as a host of fashion, jewellery, shoe and gift shops. For one-off shops and designer boutiques, **Manuka** is the place to be. For arts and crafts and tempting food stalls, head to the **Old Bus Depot Markets** (*Wentworth Avenue, Kingston; Sun 1000–1600*).

Nightlife

Canberra has some good pubs and a strong music and arts scene. See the *Canberra Times* entertainment section on Thursday or the free *bma* magazine.

Pubs to try include the Irish theme pub, **P.J. O'Reillys** (*cnr West Row and Alinga St*), which has bands on Saturday nights. Across the way is the **Wig & Pen**, which serves real ale and brews its own beer. Named after a 1940s' Sydney madame, **Tilley Devine's** (*cnr Brigalow & Wattle Sts, Lyneham; tel: (02) 6247 7753*) is a bar/coffee shop/restaurant and small music venue, revered for its repertoire of big-name ticketed shows and free musicians' practice nights. The atmosphere is friendly and tolerant, the dark wood and velvet décor breathe faded opulence, the people are of all ages and persuasions. The **Liquid Lounge** night club in Petrie Plaza has karaoke (Thur), retro (Fri), dance (Sat) and HiNRG (Sun). The **Canberra Theatre Centre** (*Civic Square; tel: (02) 6257 1077*) has several theatres showcasing performing arts from dance and opera to drama and classical music.

PROFILE
Festivals

Wherever you go in NSW and the ACT, local festivals abound with music, fireworks, craft stalls and street performers or lively celebrations of a specific aspect of a region or town such as flowers, wine, poetry, art or even the beach.

Canberra

One of Canberra's main festivals is the month-long Floriade, a floral celebration from mid September in the lakeside Commonwealth Park of over 1.3 million bulbs and annuals. From March to May, there's Canberra's Season of Festivals, which encompasses dance, music and multicultural events. In April, the National Folk Festival takes place in Exhibition Park, as well as the Chamber Music Festival at various venues. Later on in the year, the Festival of Contemporary Arts takes place in October.

Elsewhere in NSW

December
Carols by candlelight events all over NSW.

January
Sydney Festival – a month-long jamboree of drama, chamber music, visual arts, open-air cinema and recitals.

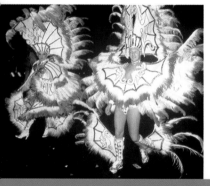

Tamworth Country Music Festival – a ten-day celebration with country music in clubs, streets, pubs and parks.

February
The Gay and Lesbian Mardi Gras – a month-long celebration of gay and lesbian culture, culminating in a parade and all-night party (*see pages 66–67*).

May

Sydney Writers Festival (five days) attracts Australian and international writers to present fiction (and non-fiction), poetry and drama.

Scone Horse Festival (ten days) – horse racing, equestrian events, rodeo, parades and country fêtes.

June

Sydney Film Festival (two weeks) features the best films from recent film festivals around the world, hosted at the State Theatre.

Yulefest – Christmas comes early in the Blue Mountains with roast turkey, carol singing and festive trimmings from June to August.

August

City to Surf Run – a fun run from Sydney's Town Hall to Bondi Beach

Bellingen Jazz Festival (*see page 119*). (*see page 119*)

September

Carnivale, a three-week-long multicultural festival of music and dance, is celebrated throughout most of NSW.

Festival of the Winds (second Sunday): kites fly high over Bondi, alongside wandering performers and multicultural music and dance.

October

Manly Jazz Festival – a huge international jazz festival with indoor and outdoor venues.

Jacaranda Festival, Grafton (*see page 127*). (*see page 127*)

The Hunter Valley vineyards (particularly Tyrells and Wyndhams) run a programme of jazz and opera 'in the vines'.

Bellingen's Global Festival (October long weekend) includes traditional, classical and contemporary music and dance.

> Beyond the horizon . . . a great, creative impulse is at work – the only thing that gives this continent meaning and a guarantee of the future. Every Australian ought to climb up here . . . and glimpse the various, manifold life of which he is a part.

Vance Palmer, Australian novelist

Lifestyles

Shopping, eating, children and nightlife in New South Wales

MANORS

LIFESTYLES

Shopping

Shopping in New South Wales is infinitely varied. Large shopping malls – in Sydney's Pitt St, Canberra, Coffs Harbour and Port Macquarie – house everything from homewares to fashions under one roof. Weekend markets – Bondi, Paddington, the Rocks and the north coast markets around Byron Bay – offer great opportunities to pick up alternative souvenirs with a twist of hippie chic. Glorious galleries, filled with Australian art the colour of the sea and sun, nestle in rural backwaters. Label fanatics can indulge in credit card heaven in Castlereagh St, Sydney's 'golden mile'. Whatever your budget, there's plenty to choose from and much that is different and unusual.

State-wide stores

There are several discount department stores such as **Woolworths**, **BigW** and **Target**, which sell everything from CDs and books to homewares and stationery at cheap prices. At the exclusive end of the scale is **David Jones** (*65–77 Market St/86–108 Castlereagh St, Sydney; Canberra Centre, Canberra*) and one notch down, **Grace Brothers** (*Pitt St Mall, Sydney; Canberra Centre, Canberra*), which offer a superb selection of clothes, sportswear and homewares. David Jones's food hall is the Harrods of Sydney, second to none in variety and quality. For ordinary food shopping, **Coles** or **Franklins** supermarkets are everywhere.

Bargain buys

If you're low on funds, the factory outlets on floor two of **Market City** sell cut-price items from mainstream names such as Osh Kosh B'Gosh children's clothes, Guess casual wear, Events and Esprit women's fashions, Nine West shoes and bags, Ray-Ban glasses and brightly coloured clothes by the Sydney artist, Ken Done.

The **Byron Bay Arts and Industry Estate** is home to wholesale businesses and craft showrooms, where prices are considerably cheaper. Look out for **Byron Designworks** (*3 Ti-Tree Place*) for homewares and **Colin Heaney's** glass-blowing gallery (*9 Acacia St*).

South Sea pearls, from the west coast are some of the finest in the world. Western Australia's gold is good value and comes in 9 or 18 carats.

Sydney's King and Castlereagh Sts jewellers drip chandeliers of gemstones – but the prices have at least three noughts. Try **Paspaley Pearls** (*142 King St*), or **Hardy Brothers** (*Skygarden, 77 Castlereagh St*) if diamonds are your best friend. For a milder shock to the system, check out the **QVB** and **Strand Arcade**. **Sydney's Dinosaur Designs** (*Strand Arcade/339 Oxford St, Paddington*) specialises in ultra trendy, brightly coloured, chunky jewellery made from translucent resin.

Shopping customs

Prices are fixed in shops and even at markets haggling is rare unless you're buying several things from the same stall, when you might be able to knock off a few dollars. Many tourist-orientated stores, such as Australian souvenir, jewellery and fashion shops, offer tax-free shopping. To benefit you will need to show your airline ticket and passport.

What to buy

Jewellery

Australia's rich mining territories provide 90 per cent of the world's opals. The most valuable are red on black, but there are many variations. They're on sale everywhere, although the **Sydney Rocks** is famed for its opal jewellers. Make sure you pick a solid gemstone, not a doublet or triplet, which are thin veneers of opal magnified by a quartz dome. Sapphires are also good quality, and

Fashion

Fashions in NSW range from the high-street casual to boutique chic, with many Australian designers gaining an international following. For affordable high-street fashion, popular chain stores include Sussans, Sportsgirl, Katies, Events, Jag and Jeans West. Upmarket Australian designers to look out for are Carla Zampatti, Anthea Crawford, Saba and Collette Dinnigan (particularly for lingerie). For one-off creations by NSW's up-and-coming fashion gurus, head to the **Fashion Emporium** in Paddington. But if only the flashiest internationally recognised labels will do, get yourself down to Sydney's **MLC Centre** and surrounding streets for a quick fix of Armani, Louis Vuitton, Bulgari and their budget-busting counterparts.

167

Designer heaven also awaits in Sydney's upmarket eastern suburb, **Double Bay**.

At the other end of the scale, **Paddington's Saturday market** and **Canberra's Kingston Bus Depot Market** (*Wentworth Ave*) on Sundays are good starting-points for reasonably priced handmade jumpers, cute children's outfits and quality second-hand clothing. For beach wear, bikinis, sarongs and the super-trendy Quiksilver, RipCurl and Mambo surf gear, **Byron Bay** is difficult to beat.

For fashion statements that scream Australia, the stores to look out for are **R M Williams**, which specialises in 'bush clothing' such as moleskin trousers and riding boots, and **Driza-Bone**, which sells oiled jackets and coats. For bushwalkers, **Akubra** hats with their sun-beating-off brims are an essential purchase. The excellent, olde worlde **Strand Hatters** in the Sydney arcade of the same name is a good starting-point.

Art and crafts

Australia has a burgeoning art and crafts scene, with the best buys in olde worlde colonial towns and villages, which lend themselves perfectly to browsing afternoons. Recent years have seen a move away from the dull greens and reds that characterised colonial art towards the bright blues, yellows and oranges that reflect the colours of Australia's vibrant landscape. Pottery and ceramics are great value ranging in style from chunky earthenware bowls to refined, lacquer noodle dishes.

Arts and crafts are a major focus for tiny towns such as **Berrima, Byron** and **Bellingen**, but even one-donkey villages such as **Bundanoon** and **Nimbin** have at least one wonderful gallery. Countryside craft shops pop up all over the place, attached to motorway service stations and cafés as well as tourist attractions.

Unsurprisingly, arty souvenirs tend to be significantly cheaper outside Sydney, particularly along the north coast, at country markets around Byron, and in Bellingen, where you can buy directly from the artists' workshops at the Old Butter Factory. One exception to this is the **Laughing Museum** (*16 Elizabeth St, Paddington*), where the sculptures (if you're into body parts) are very reasonably priced. Bellingen's **Yellow Shed** also offers a tremendous variety of inspired arts and crafts, plus some interesting books.

Junk shops abound in out-of-the-way places, full of farm implements, commemorative tins, battered jewellery, old pots – the phrase 'One man's meat is another man's poison' often springs to mind. One such junk shop adjoins the pretty **Plough Inn** at **Wingen** (near Burning Mountain). At the other end of the spectrum, the leafy **Queen St** in **Woollahra** (the suburb next to Paddington) is home to expensive antique shops.

Aboriginal art is increasing in popularity and distinctive handpainted pottery, ceremonial seed and bean necklaces, animal carvings, statues, traditional paintings, boomerangs and beautifully decorated didgeridoos are widely available. Many galleries have an aboriginal section, but there are several specialist galleries in Sydney. Check out **Blue Gum Designs** and **New Guinea Primitive Arts** (*in the QVB*), or the **Hogarth Gallery/Aboriginal Art Centre** (*7 Walker Lane, Paddington, closed Sun–Mon*) for more serious collectors. If you head to Jervis Bay, pop into **Laddie's Aboriginal Shop** (*at the Lady Denman Complex, Huskisson*).

169

Food and drink

Anyone arriving in Australia expecting a slab of beef on the barbecue, swilled down with a bucket of beer, is in for a pleasant surprise. Despite the stereotyping, Australian cuisine is very cosmopolitan, particularly in Sydney, Canberra and the larger coastal towns.

Styles of food

Australia opened its doors to immigrants from Europe after World War II, leading to strong Mediterranean influences in the national cuisine. The influx of immigrants from Asia, Africa and South America made a similar mark in the 1970s and 1980s. Consequently, what has become known as **modern Australian cuisine** is a distinctive blend of Pacific and Mediterranean flavours, with a strong leaning towards clean, fresh tastes.

However, the immigrant populations have also established their own **ethnic** restaurants. More than a quarter of Sydney's residents were born overseas, and the city has large Lebanese, Greek, Spanish, Italian and Chinese communities. Authentic Chinese is plentiful in Chinatown at Haymarket, Spanish restaurants cluster around Liverpool St, near Darling Harbour, whilst Oxford St, Victoria St and Kings Cross play host to cuisines from all corners of the globe.

Over the last few years, 'bush tucker' has become fashionable, with native aboriginal foods such as berries, seeds and herbs creeping on to menus in the form of bush tomatoes, lemon myrtle and Illawarra plums.

On the menu

Australian seafood tends to be exceptional and specialist restaurants are plentiful, particularly in Sydney and along the coast. Dishes to try are **barramundi**, a large tropical fish with delicate white flesh, the heavier, slightly oily **jewfish**, the flat, round **John Dory**, with firm, white flesh or the light, delicately flavoured **mahi mahi**. Shellfish enthusiasts will enjoy **Moreton Bay Bugs** (a saltwater crustacean from the Brisbane region), **Sydney Rock Oysters** and freshwater crayfish, known as 'yabbies', as well as the wonderfully succulent **lobster**, **king prawns** and **blue swimmer crab**.

Meat in NSW is extremely good and inexpensive. NSW's milk-fed **lamb** is particularly tender and all manner of **beef** from steaks to roasts is very tasty. Many restaurants, and particularly pubs, will offer meat simply chargrilled, others will dress it up with a variety of sauces. The **barbecue** is still a prominent feature of Aussie life and most national parks, popular beaches and picnic spots have a barbecue area where you can cook your own. In some restaurants, they supply the meat for you to cook on a communal barbie, which is great fun, not least because Australians vie with each other to share their barbecuing wisdom with visitors! Other tasty alternatives include low-fat, low-cholesterol **kangaroo**, **emu** and **crocodile**.

Fruit and vegetables are extremely varied, benefiting from the sunny orchards of NSW rather than the hothouse conditions of cooler countries. Look out for the delicious **sun-roasted tomatoes**, rich green **rocket salad** leaves and exotic **tropical fruits** available all year round.

171

Eating out

Breakfast is a celebrated part of the day, with many workers starting their day at their neighbourhood café, enjoying frothy coffee, freshly squeezed juices, muffins, pancakes or even a fry up. **Lunchtime** *fare revolves around soups, salads and doorstopping focaccias – Italian olive-oil bread with a variety of Mediterranean toppings. Shopping malls usually have a large food court with take-away counters ranging from Italian, Chinese and Thai to Indian, seafood and organic dishes, eaten in a large communal area.*

Picnic fans can turn upmarket in the wonderful delis dotted about NSW: **cheese-tasting rooms** are becoming popular. The combination of the cheese of your choice and the other delicacies on offer – prosciutto, stuffed olives, sun-dried tomatoes, humus, king prawns – makes for a gourmet feast. **Bakeries** sell a mind-blowing choice of bread – rye, pitta, baguette, coffee and date, muesli, mustard and cheese twirls – plus calorific meat pies and pasties for traditional die-hards. **Markets** provide an excellent opportunity to stock up on eucalyptus honey, macadamia nuts and locally harvested fruit.

Restaurants vary enormously in price and setting – anywhere with a waterfront/beach view is likely to be on the pricey side. Cheaper restaurants nestle alongside exclusive ones, so don't be put off if you find yourself in a swanky area. All except the most upmarket restaurants have relaxed dress codes – ie no tie or jacket. Restaurants in NSW encompass everything from the fast-food hamburger chains to beach cafés, fun informal bistros, pub food and formal, linen tablecloth, fine dining. Restaurants in cities are usually open at least six days a week and often seven. Eateries in country areas may be closed on Monday or Tuesday. Lunch is generally served 1230–1430 and dinner 1830–2230 (2130 in country areas). Many

restaurants in seaside areas offer weekend brunches 1000–1600. It's a good idea to book for popular restaurants.

One of the best quirky elements of Australian restaurant culture is the BYO phenomenon. Many restaurants are unlicensed and encourage you to bring your own wine or beer to drink with your meal for a negligible corkage charge. There will almost always be a bottle shop (off licence/liquor store) near by. This practice keeps the restaurant bill down, with the added bonus of being able to drink great wines at supermarket prices. Some licensed restaurants also allow you to BYO for a slightly increased corkage fee.

Drinks

Coffee is complex in Australia. It comes in a variety of forms – flat white (milky coffee), short black (espresso), cappuccino, caffe latte and more. Smoothies are popular daytime drinks – thick milkshakes with real fruit – and freshly squeezed fruit juices such as carrot and ginger

are definitely in. Fizzy drinks such as coke and lemonade are available everywhere, although sparkling mineral water is the exception rather than the rule.

Australians are big beer drinkers. Beer is served very cold. One of the most common beers in the state is VB (Victoria Bitter) which, despite its name, is similar to British lager. Toohey's is the largest NSW brewer – look out for Toohey's Draught. Other popular brews include Carlton Cold, Hahn Ice, Reschs and Coopers. Low-alcohol beers have become increasingly popular owing to the stringent drink–driving laws and most major breweries produce 'light' versions of mainstream beers. A small beer is a 'middy', a large beer is a 'schooner'.

Australian wine is so good that imported wines are usually reserved for only the finest wine lists. Hunter Valley wines are excellent, although you should try out bottles from other wine-producing regions such as South Australia and Victoria too. A pleasant wine can easily cost less than $10 and $15–$20 will buy you a really good bottle. Semillon, Chardonnay and a blend of the two are popular whites, whilst reds tend to be Cabernet Sauvignon, Shiraz and blends of several grape varieties. All spirits are widely available, although rum, from Queensland, is a particular speciality – look out for the dark Bundaberg rum.

173

Children's activities

Sydney and NSW generally are easy destinations to enjoy as a family. There's no shortage of beaches, parks and child-friendly museums in the city, whilst out in the country the national parks have wildlife on tap – kangaroos, parrots, emus – plus a myriad of dolphin cruises to delight even the sulkiest teenager.

Sydney

Museums, zoos and aquariums

Museums in Sydney have eschewed the 'look and label' approach in favour of vibrant interactive displays. Children love the dinosaurs and the displays of hairy spiders and slippery snakes at the **Australian Museum** (*pages 56–57*), the spine-tingling sharks and touch pools at the **Sydney Aquarium** (*page 40*) or **Manly Oceanworld** (*page 75*), and the beauties and the beasts at **Taronga Zoo** (*page 79*). The **National Maritime Museum** (*page 42*) runs special children's events such as swashbuckling pirate musicals and all-night sleepovers on the HMAS *Vampire* during the school holidays (*for information tel: (02) 9552 7777*), whilst the **Powerhouse Museum** (*pages 42–43*) has locomotives to clamber on, space shuttles to explore and lots of interactive technology to play with.

Darling Harbour

Darling Harbour is a haven for children – they can play in the water features, ride on the trackless **'People Mover'** train, watch the street performers or dress in elaborate costumes and fancy headdresses (*open 1000–1700; $*) in the **Chinese Tea Gardens** (*page 41*). For the footsore, the **IMAX Cinema** shows nature and action films in 3-D (with the aid of liquid crystal glasses) on screens ten times the normal size (*daily on the hour, every hour, 1000–2200; tel (02) 9281 3300 for programme details; $$*). **Sega World** (*1–25 Harbour St; tel: (02) 9273 9273; open Mon–Fri 1100–2200, Sat–Sun 1000–2200*) is a virtual reality, hi-tech theme park, with rollercoasters, interactive space missions and haunted houses, and time travel between past, present and future zones. A ride on the **monorail** (*page 16*) is an enjoyable way for them to see over Sydney.

Outdoor activities

A day at the beach (Bondi, Bronte) is always fun for children and a ferry ride (to Watson's Bay or Manly) makes it even more enjoyable. Ensure that your children swim between the flags at all times.

Bondi's skateboard basin, Centennial Park and the seafront at Manly all offer a suitable playground for rollerbladers and skateboarders.

Out and about

Attractions outside Sydney include the country's answer to Disneyland, **Australia's Wonderland** (*Wallgrove Rd, Eastern Creek; tel: (02) 9830 9100/toll free 1800 252 198; open daily; $$$*) with over 80 rides, a wildlife park and outback woolshed. Take the M4 west out of Sydney and follow signs or go by City Rail to Rooty Hill, then shuttle bus.

Port Macquarie offers the **Koala Hospital** (*page 105*) plus two theme parks:

Fantasy Glades (*Parklands Close, off Pacific Drive; tel: (02) 6582 2506; open daily 0900–1700; $*), which is an imagination-inspiring medley of enchanted forests, Snow White's diamond mine, Cinderella's castle, and crooked houses; and **Peppermint Park** (*cnr Pacific Drive and Ocean St; tel: (02) 6583 6111; open Tue– Sun 1000–1700, daily in school holidays; $$*), which has everything for fun in the sun from water slides to go-karts, swings, giant skipping ropes, crazy golf and a rollerblading area, plus resident monkeys and an aviary.

A few kilometres away at **Wauchope** is the 14m-high fibreglass **Big Bull** (*Redbank Farm, Redbank Rd; tel: (02) 6585 2044; open daily 1000–1600; $*). This is the brainchild of Farmer John, who will take you on a tractor tour around the farm, followed by a visit to the nursery where geese and goats, puppies and lambs all exist in complete harmony.

The coast from Port Stephens to Byron Bay offers **dolphin- and whale-spotting** cruises (*see individual chapters*), whilst further south, **Canberra**'s child-friendly activities include the **Questacon Science and Technology Centre** (*page 158*) and **Tidbinbilla Nature Reserve** (*page 159*), as well as boating on the lake and cycling around it on a tandem (*page 152*).

After dark

Whether you want post-dinner drinks to a background of mellow music, a night at the ballet or an energetic dance to the loudest, latest techno beats, Sydney's after-dark entertainment offers something for everyone. There's also a wide variety of free street entertainment, ranging from lunchtime concerts in the city centre to roving performers around the Rocks and Darling Harbour.

Finding out what's on

The Metro section of Friday's *Sydney Morning Herald* lists cultural and fun events on around the city. Free magazines such as *3DWorld*, *Beat* and *On the Street* offer a guide to the latest gig, club, film and music events. The *Sydney Arts and Cultural Guide* (free from tourist information centres), is an excellent bi-annual guide to the best of Sydney's performing arts, galleries and exhibitions, with seating plans of the main theatres, a help when booking seats by phone. Bookings for most events can be made through **Ticketek** (*tel: (02) 9266 4800*) and **Ticketmaster** (*tel: (02) 9320 9000*).

Nightclubs

Oxford St (and close environs) is the clubbing mecca of Sydney, with a few good dance venues in the city centre. Many are exceptionally trendy and in some places, the fashion police at the door decide who's in and who's out – so no jeans. Most have one night (or several) a week which are particularly gay-friendly, plus themed music nights so it pays to check in advance. Some are free, others have moderate entry fees, rarely more than the cost of a round of drinks.

Bentley Bar

320 Crown St, Surry Hills. Tel: (02) 9331 1186. Open daily, early afternoon to the early hours. This small, sweaty bar plays dance music every night for trendy young straights (gay night is Tuesday). It's a popular

post-midnight venue when revellers head here to continue partying to a mixture of house, garage and UK charts with in-house DJs.

Club Retro

Angle Place (cnr or Pitt St). Tel: (02) 9223 2220. Open Fri and Sat 2000–0300. $$. Head down here and watch the years roll back to the 1980s with Spandau Ballet, ABC and Human League gyrating on massive video screens.

DCM

33 Oxford St, Darlinghurst. Tel: (02) 9267 7380. Open Thur–Fri 2300– late, Sat 2200–1100, Sun 2300– 0730. $–$$. Just queuing for hours doesn't guarantee you entry into DCM. The best trendy gear is *de rigueur* for a chance to dance on the podiums at this large super-hip club, with top Australian DJs and a very

beautiful, mixed hetero-homo crowd. Drag shows and camp cabarets feature, particularly on a Thursday.

Sublime

244 Pitt St, Central Business District. Tel: (02) 9264 8428. Open Fri 1630–0500, Sat 2300–0700, Sun 2200–0500. $$. A top hang-out for serious clubbers (and the best air-con in town), the music is hard house and dance, the gyrating bodies a mixture of outrageous lycra outfits and nightclubbers' black.

Other venues worth checking out for one-off all night party events are the Dendy at 19 Martin Place and the Skygarden Pub at the top of the Skygarden shopping mall.

Cinemas

Multi-screen cinemas line the section of George St between Liverpool and Bathurst Sts, showing new releases and mainstream films. Try the six-screen Greater Union (*525 George St; tel: (02) 9267 8666/recorded info: 133 456*) or the barn-like Hoyts (*505 George St; tel: (02) 9273 7431/recorded info: 132 700*). Alternative, foreign films and a few mainstream movies are on show at the Dendy (*19 Martin Place; tel: (02) 9233 8166*). A mixture of arty alternatives, blockbusters and all-time favourites show at the Movie Room (*112 Darlinghurst Rd; tel: (02) 9380 5162*), where for a couple

❝ *Remember you're here to sweat and look fabulous so you want that fabric to cling to your butt like fungus.* **❞**

Sydney Sidewalk website review of DCM club

177

of bucks more than your average cinema ticket, your entry fee includes a dinner at **Govinda's** veggie restaurant below. Most cinemas offer cut-price tickets on Tuesdays.

Live music venues

The Basement

29 Reiby Place, between Pitt and Loftus Sts. Tel: (02) 9251 2797. Open Mon–Fri lunchtimes plus happy hour 1630–1830, daily for dinner and shows, 1930–late. $–$$. The best jazz venue in Sydney. The performers range from international greats to local jazz, country and blues artists making mellow music. Evening shows start around 2100, so you can have dinner in the bistro first. Book for a stage-side table.

The Entertainment Centre

Harbour St, Haymarket. Tel: (02) 9320 4200, info line 1800 957 333, tickets (02) 9266 4800. Has seating for 12,000 and hosts massive pop concerts and big-name rock bands.

The Rocks

Many pubs in the Rocks' George St – the Mercantile, Fortune of War, The Orient – have live bands most evenings and on Sunday afternoons.

Harbourside Brasserie

Pier One, Dawes Point. Tel: (02) 9252 3000. $$–$$$. Enjoy dinner (served until 2300) to a backdrop of blues, soul and funk played by mainly local performers.

Classical and opera

Sydney has a very strong classical music scene. Names to look out for are the **Australian Chamber Orchestra** (*tel: (02) 9357 4111, www.aco.com.au*), **Musica Viva** (*tel: (02) 9698 1711, www.mva.org.au*), one of the world's largest chamber music organisations, and **Sydney Symphony Orchestra** (*tel: (02) 9334 4600*). The Concert Hall at the Opera House is a favourite venue for all three. **Opera Australia** (*tel: gen enquiries (02) 9319 3333/booking (02) 9319 1088*) offers an innovative programme at Sydney's Opera House. Keep an eye open for special events linked to the Sydney Festival in January, such as outdoor jazz, symphony and opera in the Domain.

Theatres

Sydney Opera House

Bennelong Point. Box office open Mon–Sat 0900–2030. Tel: (02) 9250 7777. This is a good starting-point for cultural events which range

from opera, ballet and drama, to dance, pop and symphony concerts.

Wharf Theatre

Pier 4, Hickson Rd, Walsh Bay. Tel: (02) 9250 1777/enquiries (02) 9250 1700. Excellent drama performed by the city's prestigious Sydney Theatre Company.

The Lyric Theatre

20–80 Pyrmont Rd, Star City. Tel: (02) 9777 9000. Opened in 1997, this state-of-the-art theatre favours international productions and musicals of the Showboat variety.

State Theatre

49 Market St. Tel: (02) 9373 6655/ advance bookings Ticketmaster (02) 9320 9000. It's worth going to see whatever is on here for the fabulously opulent, chandelier-studded interior. It hosts the Sydney Film Festival, many pop concerts and musicals.

Capitol Theatre (*13 Campbell St, Haymarket; tel: (02) 9230 5000*) and **Theatre Royal** (*MLC Centre, King St, City Centre; tel: (02) 9224 8444*) are home to ballets, musicals and major international productions.

Dance and theatre

The Australian Ballet and the city's leading contemporary dance group, the Sydney Dance Company (*tel: (02) 9221 4811,*

www.sydneydance.com.au) both perform at the Sydney Opera House (*tel: (02) 9250 7777*). The Sydney Theatre Company favours its own **Wharf Theatre** (*tel: (02) 9250 1777*), as well as Opera House theatres for contemporary British and American plays and the latest from popular Australian playwrights.

Out of town

Elsewhere in New South Wales, nightlife other than pubs and restaurants can be thin on the ground. **Byron Bay** has good live music venues such as the Beach Hotel, the Rails and the Great Northern Hotel. In the Snowy Mountains, **Thredbo** rocks till late during the ski season at the Schuss Bar and Keller Bar in the Alpine Hotel. Live music in **Coffs Harbour** centres around the **Coffs Ex-Services Club** (*Vernon St; tel: (02) 6652 3888*) with big names at the **RSL** in Sawtell (*tel: (02) 6653 1577*).

RSL

Towns, and often quite small villages, all over NSW have RSL clubs, which put on concerts, dances and films at low prices, subsidised by money made from the poker machines. They are often members only, but most will allow entry to overseas visitors on production of a passport or driving licence (phone beforehand).

Practical
information

CRUISES

ROSE BAY WATSONS BAY

McMahons Point
Milsons Point
Cremorne Point
Darling Point
Double Bay
Rose Bay
Watsons Bay

WHARF

NEUTRAL BAY

Kirribilli
High to North Sydney
*Hacto to Neutral Bay
Kurraba Point

HARBOUR BEACHES

Transfer at Manly for:
Balmoral
Quarantine Station
Watsons Bay

WHARF WHARF

MOSMAN

Cremorne Point
Taronga Zoo
Mosman to Mosman South
Old Cremorne
Arrival to Mosman

ZOO to to

Taronga Zoo
Cremorne Point

WHARF WHARF

MANLY

Manly FERRY

Manly JETCAT

WHARF WHARF

You are now on Wharf No. 5

Tickets

...tacular Aquarium

PRACTICAL INFORMATION

Practical information

Airports

International flights arrive at Sydney's **Kingsford Smith** airport, where there is an information desk on arrivals level one, as well as major car rental companies and money change facilities. The airport is only 9km south of the city centre and the quickest way into the city is by taxi from the rank outside the terminal. The

journey takes 20–30 minutes and costs about three times as much as the bus. The green and gold **Airport Express** (*tel: 131 500; operates 0500–2300*) runs a cheap, regular service between domestic and international terminals, and the city centre and Kings Cross. Route 300 runs to Circular Quay, George St and Central station, whilst route 350 takes passengers to Kings Cross via Central station and Oxford St. The journey can take up to an hour. Family tickets for two adults and any number of children are available. **Kingsford Smith Bus Service** and **Sydney Hotel/Motel** provide an inexpensive half-hourly shuttle service to and from the airport (*daily 0500–1800*), with stops at selected hotels in the city centre, Kings Cross, Glebe, Double Bay and Darling Harbour. The cheapest option is the service operated by **Sydney Bus**, which links the airport to Railway Square and Central station (*bus 305, every 30 minutes, peak hours only,*

Mon–Fri), to the northern beaches (*bus 100*) and to Bondi (*bus 400*).

Climate

Seasons in Australia are the opposite to the northern hemisphere. Unlike some states, NSW has four distinct seasons, with Sydney enjoying a mild and temperate climate. Summer runs from December to February, ushering in outdoor cinema and open-air concerts, along with beachfront barbecues and shady picnics in Sydney's parks. However, some days can be hot and humid with temperatures spiralling into the 30s, sending Sydneysiders scuttling up the coast at weekends to Port Stephens or to the cool of the Blue Mountains. Autumn (Mar–May) is the wettest time, when the wind gets up and temperatures stay around 20°C (68°F). Average winter temperatures from June to August are 15°C (59°F), occasionally plunging to a 7°C (45°F) low. Spring is the prettiest time of all, when the countryside unfurls into a carpet of wildflowers and, despite a chill in the air, the months from September to November usually see sunny days. The temperature creeps up the further up the coast you go, with the southern regions coolest of all. The ski season in the Snowy Mountains in the south runs from June to October.

Currency

The Australian currency is the dollar, which is divided into 100 cents. Notes are plasticised, and come in $5 (purple), $10 (blue), $20 (orange), $50 (yellow) and $100 (green) denominations. Coins include 5c, 10c, 50c, $1 and $2. Travellers' cheques will generally be accepted in large hotels, otherwise they should be changed in a bank (take your passport). Credit cards are widely accepted, although their use in smaller towns and country areas is more restricted. The most popular are American Express, Visa, MasterCard, Diner's Club and Bankcard. Credit cards and ordinary bankcards bearing an international symbol such as Cirrus, plus PIN number, can be used to withdraw cash from ATMs, which operate 24 hours a day. High street banks with branches throughout the state include Westpac, ANZ, National Australia Bank and Commonwealth Bank.

Customs regulations

Travellers arriving in Australia need to complete a customs declaration form, which is handed in at immigration. Apart from the usual bans on bringing in plants and animals, you cannot bring in any fresh food. Passengers over 18 can bring in 1125ml alcohol and 250 cigarettes or 250g tobacco duty free, plus $400 worth of gifts ($200 for people under 18). There's no limit to how much currency you can bring into Australia, although more than A$10,000 or the foreign currency equivalent must be declared on arrival. This total doesn't include travellers' cheques.

Disabled travellers

Provision for disabled travellers is generally good in the main cities. Many museums, cinemas, theatres and tourist hot-spots have wheelchair facilities, although public transport remains a challenge. Some RiverCat ferries and ferries to Manly have ramped access, and the wharves at Manly and Circular Quay are wheelchair accessible. The two main bodies that provide information for the disabled are **NICAN**, which offers information on recreation, tourism, sport and the arts, and **ACROD**, the national industry association of disability services. They can be contacted as follows:

NICAN: *PO Box 407, Curtin, ACT 2605. Tel: (02) 6285 3713. E-mail: nican@spirit.com.au* **ACROD**: *33 Thesiger Court, Deakin, ACT 2600. Tel: (02) 6281 3488.*

Publications:
Easy Access Australia – A Travel Guide to Australia by Bruce Cameron (Easy Access Australia Publishing ISBN 0646-25581-9): this comprehensive guide contains information on accessible accommodation, tourist facilities and general tourist information.

Accessing Sydney: A handbook for people with disabilities and those who have problems getting around, by ACROD NSW (ISBN: 0-646-21255-9), is a useful guide to the city.

Internet sites:
Easy Access Australia – 'A Travel Guide to Australia' *www.vicnet.net.au/~bruceeaa* The Australian Tourist Commission's website (www.australia.com) also has a wide range of information under the special interest section.

Wheelchair accessible taxis:
Sydney: **Zero 200** (*tel: 1800 043 187*). Canberra: **Aerial taxis** (*tel: (02) 6285 9222*).

Electricity

Australia's electrical current is 220–240 volts. Plugs are flat, two or three pins (not the same as the British three-pin varieties), so most travellers will need an adaptor plug. Most hotels have 240 and 110 volts shaver sockets.

Entry formalities

All visitors to Australia must have a valid passport and, with the exception of New Zealand passport-holders, a visa issued in their own country. In 1996, the Electronic Travel Authority (ETA) was introduced. This is an 'invisible' visa. Your details are entered onto travel-industry booking systems without any form-filling or stamps in your passport. The visa is verified when you check in for your flight and when you arrive in Australia. Visitors from the UK, Ireland, Canada, US and most Western European countries can apply for an ETA through airline reservation offices and participating travel agents and, in most cases, it is granted instantly. Tourist visas for stays of up to three months each over a 12-month period are free, although individual travel agents may make an administration charge if you haven't booked the holiday through them. Longer stays and business visas incur a processing fee. Visitors from countries which do not participate in the ETA scheme must apply for a visa from their nearest Australian consulate. South Africans can apply to the **Australian High Commission** (*292 Orient St (cnr Schoeman St), Arcadia, Pretoria 0083; tel: (012) 342 3740*). For ETA services, contact **Rennies Travel** in Johannesburg (*tel: (011) 407 3343*), Cape Town (*tel: (021) 418 5626*) or Durban (*tel: (011) 304 9971*).

Health

Australia has excellent medical facilities and a good national health insurance scheme called **Medicare**. Visitors from New Zealand, the UK, Ireland, Malta, Sweden, Italy, Finland and the Netherlands are eligible, under a reciprocal agreement, for free emergency medical and hospital treatment. To exercise this right, you need to register at any local Medicare office (look in the Yellow Pages). Dental treatment, ambulance services or repatriation in case of injury or illness aren't covered, so health insurance is still a good idea, and an absolute necessity for anyone from countries not included in the agreement. No vaccinations are needed for entry into Australia unless you have visited a yellow-fever-infected area within six days prior to your arrival in Australia.

Health hazards

Australia has its fair share of bronzed sun gods and goddesses, but the high incidence of skin cancer means that many people stay relatively pale. Overseas visitors should protect themselves from the strong Aussie sun by wearing a long-sleeved T-shirt and a wide-brimmed hat and applying a hefty dose of factor 15-plus water-resistant sun-tan lotion. Make sure you drink plenty of water and keep out of the sun 1100–1500 during daylight saving (end of October–end of March) and 1000–1400 at other times.

Another common hazard for visitors, particularly those unused to ocean beaches, are the rips and undertows. To put it into perspective, the lifeguards who patrol most of the popular beaches around Sydney pull out an average of

11,000 people a year. Red and yellow flags mark safe swimming areas up and down the coast, and you should always try to swim between them. If you do get into trouble, don't try to swim against the current, float with it and raise your arm for help.

Bush fires are very common in the summer. Indicators along the road show the fire risk for the day. Some days are designated 'total fire ban' days, which means exactly that – no barbies, no camping stoves – and never throw cigarettes out of the car window on any day. Fires spread like lightning, so leave the area as soon as you see smoke, even if it's in the distance. If you're planning a camping trip or setting off on a long bushwalk, phone the **Country Fire Authority** (*tel: 131 599*) to check on conditions.

Despite Australia's deserved reputation for poisonous spiders and snakes, it's quite possible that you will finish your trip without bumping into one, poisonous or otherwise. You are very unlikely to be bitten, but sturdy boots when bushwalking are a good idea. Be careful when gathering wood for barbecues, and never put your hand into crevices or tree hollows. If you are bitten, seek urgent medical attention – antidotes are available for most bites.

Information

You're never far away from an information source in Australia. These can range from well-equipped official centres with books, leaflets and maps to volunteer-run kiosks overflowing with helpful advice, to cafés, newsagents or junk stores in small towns with a couple of dog-eared leaflets and lots of local charm. Wherever you end up, it's usually a friendly and helpful experience, particularly when run by volunteers.

Some of the popular national parks and nature reserves, such as Dorrigo, Tidbinbilla and Morton, have visitor centres, others are limited to a couple of walking trail and wildlife information boards.

The main information centre for Sydney and NSW is the **Sydney Visitor Centre** (*106 George St, The Rocks; tel: (02) 9255 1788*). For advice on state-wide accommodation and travel visit the **NSW Travel Centre** (*11–17 York St; tel: 132 077*). Wildlife lovers and walkers should pop into **National Parks and Wildlife Service (NPWS) Information Centre** (*Cadman's Cottage, 110 George St, The Rocks; tel: (02)9247 8861*).

Regional centres include:
Snowy Region Visitor Centre: *Kosciuszko Rd, Jindabyne. Tel: (02) 6450 5600.*
The **Blue Mountains Visitor Information Centre**: *Great Western Highway, Glenbrook. Tel: (02) 4739 6266/1800 041 227.*
Hunter Valley Wine Country Information Centre: *Turner Park, Aberdare Rd, Cessnock. Tel: (02) 4990 4477.*
Great Lakes Visitors Centre: *Little St, Forster. Tel: (02) 65 54 879.*

Publications:

The *Sydney Morning Herald* carries local, national and international news, with an arts listing in the Metro section on Fridays. A twice-yearly *Sydney Arts and Cultural Guide* (free from tourist offices) details the main events coming up over the year, whilst major happenings such as the Sydney Festival publish their own detailed guides. To find out what's in, what's out and who's wearing what, look in the bi-monthly *Fashion Journal*, available from trendy shops. Dedicated clubbers can find out what's on where in the *3DWorld* magazine, available free from clubs and bars. Canberra's free monthly entertainment guide, *bma*, is a comprehensive guide to events. An excellent series called *This Month in . . .* (Sydney, Hunter Valley, South Coast etc) is published across the state with details of what's on in each region.

Useful websites:

National Parks and Wildlife Service: *www.npws.nsw.gov.au*

Australian Tourist Commission: *www.australia.com*. This comprehensive website carries a wide range of information from maps, beaches, wildlife to what's on during your holiday dates, gay travel, honeymoons, plus details of their offices in your home country. If you can't find it on their website, there's an e-mail helpline for specific questions.

Two excellent websites contain information about Sydney ranging from restaurants to bars, clubs, attractions and nightlife: *www.citysearch.com.au* and *www.sydney.sidewalk.com.au*

Tourism New South Wales: *www.tourism.nsw.gov.au* with information about events and festivals, what to see in and around Sydney, plus museums, galleries etc.

Canberra Tourism: *www.canberratourism.com.au*

Insurance

Take out travel insurance before setting off on your trip to cover your luggage, valuables and medical care (including repatriation). If you're planning to indulge in any potentially dangerous activities such as whitewater rafting, mountain climbing, hang-gliding or skiing, make sure these are covered by your policy.

Maps

Bookstores, most petrol stations and some newsagents sell maps. However, the best starting-point is usually tourist information offices, which offer a wide range. Of the free ones, the large scale *Cartoscope Tourist Maps* are the best. There are about 15 in the series, each covering a small segment of NSW, highlighting tourist attractions. Otherwise you can usually buy good regional maps produced by either the **NRMA** (National Roads and Motorists Association) or **UBD**. Walking trail maps of the national parks are also available from tourist information centres.

Sydney is a maze of one-way streets, so you need a good city map where the traffic direction is marked. Most hired cars will come with one, otherwise the

Sydway Greater Sydney Road Atlas will stop you going round in circles. Far better to find a copy of the excellent *Sydney Public Transport Map* (available from City Rail stations and the bus kiosk behind Circular Quay), which covers buses, trains and ferries, and leave the car at home.

The Sydney Map Shop (*23–33 Bridge St, Sydney; tel: (02) 9228 6466*) sells a huge selection of touring maps, National Park maps and road directories. Information on touring, road conditions, and maps, is available from the NRMA (*151 Clarence St, Sydney; tel: 13 21 32, www.nrma.com.au*).

Opening times

Shops are generally open Mon–Fri 0900–1730, Sat 0900–1700. Sunday trading is becoming more popular with major stores open 1100–1600. Thursday is late-night shopping in Sydney until 2100. In some areas, large supermarkets such as Coles or Woolworths stay open until 2200 or midnight.

Banks are open Mon–Thur 0930–1600, Fri 0930–1700, and some open Sat morning.

Petrol stations are plentiful and are usually open seven days a week, from early till late, with shorter hours in less populated, rural areas. On major roads such as the Pacific Highway, many stay open till midnight, some are 24-hour.

Opening hours for **tourist information offices** depend on the area – official government-funded centres tend to be open daily 0900–1700, others staffed by volunteers may only be open in the mornings and closed Sun. In rural areas, information offices are often run from shops, cafés and petrol stations, so, perversely, they often stay open longer.

Businesses and offices are predominantly 9–5, weekdays only.

Restaurants are usually open seven days a week in Sydney, some close on Sun, Mon and/or Tue in quieter areas. Restaurants which depend heavily on office workers for lunchtime trade are often open for dinner only at weekends.

Pubs usually shut at 2300 during the week, midnight on Sat and 2200 on Sun, although party animals in Sydney will find no shortage of watering holes open till early morning. In rural areas, many pubs open early and close around 2130.

Major **tourist attractions** and **museums** are open daily 0900–1700, with some, such as the Sydney Aquarium, open until 2200. Less mainstream sights operate more restricted hours, typically 1000–1600 and are often closed Mon.

Church opening times vary but a rough guide is Mon–Fri 0830–1700 with slightly shorter times on Sat and slightly longer on Sun.

Public Holidays

1 Jan	New Year's Day
26 Jan	Australia Day
Third Mon in Mar (ACT only)	Canberra Day
March/April	Good Friday, Easter Saturday and Easter Monday
25 Apr	Anzac Day
Second Mon in June	Queen's Birthday
First Mon in Aug	August Bank Hol
First Mon in Oct	Labour Day
First Tue in Nov	Melbourne Cup Day – *this is not officially a holiday in NSW and ACT, but many businesses close early to watch the race.*
25 Dec	Christmas Day
26 Dec	Boxing Day

187

Reading

History

The Oxford Illustrated Dictionary of Australian History, Jan Bassett (1996, Oxford University Press Australia), is an easy, dip-in, dip-out reference book to piece together all those names and events which you've heard bandied about and feel you should know. For a comprehensive history of the colony's early days, *The Fatal Shore 1787–1868*, Robert Hughes (Collins Harvill), is an accessible read.

Walking and cycling

The best of Sydney and NSW is seen on foot or by bike. Useful guides to point you in the right direction are *Cycling the Bush – 100 Rides in NSW*, Sven Klinge and *100 Walks in NSW*, Tyrone T Thomas (both by the descriptively named Hill of Content Publishing). *Walking Sydney*, Lisa Clifford and Mandy Webb (1998, Pan Macmillan), contains 25 excellent walks around the city, with quirky anecdotes and off-beat history thrown in.

Eating out

The *Sydney Morning Herald* publishes an annual *Good Food Guide*, which is the ultimate gourmet bible, a lively, witty, sometimes scathing collection of restaurant and café reviews, heavily focused on Sydney, but with a good chunk of recommendations state-wide.

Travel writing

Sydney, Jan Morris (1992, Penguin), is a mixture of social comment, historical fact and personalities served up with perceptive insights into Sydney life, intellect, mentality and style. Her last book on Sydney back in the 1960s earned her hate-mail for five years; this one is infinitely more affectionate and entertainingly informative.

Places in the Heart (1997, Hodder Headline) is an anthology of travel 'memories', a collection of 30 prominent Australians' favourite places. Destinations include many in Australia, some in far corners of the globe. All are brought to life through childhood memories, witty anecdotes and enchanting descriptions, which offer an insight into Australian cultural values and social mores.

Safety and security

Generally, Australia has a low crime rate. However, the usual sensible precautions apply – keep to well-lit areas at night, don't flash wads of cash in public, use the safe in your hotel and keep a close eye on your wallet and handbag at all times, especially in crowded places such as Kings Cross, and on public transport. In the car, don't leave valuables on display and don't advertise the fact that you're a tourist by leaving maps and guidebooks on the seats. Visitors to small towns in rural areas will usually be welcomed, although you will also stand out like a sore thumb. Women travelling alone should book accommodation ahead and try to arrive before dark. Bear in mind that pubs in these areas tend to be fairly rough and ready and the domain of men.

Off peak, you could easily find that you have walking trails in national parks to yourself – for women in particular, it's best not to go wandering off alone. Bushwalking presents other dangers. Conditions can change very quickly and when the sun sets, it can turn very chilly. Make sure you're carrying plenty of water, sun cream, a hat plus warm clothing. If you're setting off on a long trip, check conditions first at information centres, make sure you've got a good map and tell staff your intended route.

Public transport is pretty safe. The Sydney underground has carriages designated for safe night-time travel, marked by blue lights.

If you *do* need help, the emergency number for police, fire and ambulance is 000.

Telephones

Public telephones are plentiful. Many accept coins and phone cards, others credit cards only, some take everything. Telstra phone cards ($5, $10, $20, $50) can be bought at newsagents, chemists and other retail outlets. Local calls cost a flat rate of 40c, $10 should buy you enough time to check on the dog/kids/granny back home *and* tell them where you've been. The cheapest time to call is 2200–0800, or between 1800 Saturday and 0800 on Monday.

International code: dial 0011 + country code + city code (minus initial zero) + telephone number. Country codes are (44) for the UK, (64) for New Zealand, (1) for US/Canada, (27) for South Africa.

Time

There are three time zones within Australia. New South Wales, the ACT, Victoria, Tasmania and Queensland are on eastern standard time (EST), ten hours ahead of GMT. South Australia and Northern Territories are half an hour behind EST and Western Australia is two hours behind. Daylight saving runs from the end of October to end of March, which adds an hour to the time differences. Queensland doesn't change, so check local times if you're flying north.

Tipping

Australia is a very egalitarian society and tipping is not generally expected. It's fine to tip porters, taxi drivers and hairdressers if you want to, but there's no obligation to do so. In most cafés and restaurants, it's customary to round the bill up to the nearest easy figure, although the more upmarket you go, the closer you should aim to 10 per cent.

Toilets

Public toilets are pretty thin on the ground in cities, but plentiful on the highways, in national parks and in all tourist attractions. In Sydney and elsewhere, the best conveniences are in cafés, restaurants and large department stores.

Index

191

Editorial, design and production credits

Project management: Dial House Publishing Services
Series editor: Christopher Catling
Copy editor: Posy Gosling
Proof-reader: Susie Whimster

Series and cover design: Trickett & Webb Limited
Cover artwork: Wenham Arts
Text layout: Wenham Arts
Map work: RJS Associates

Repro and image setting: Z2 Repro, Thetford, Norfolk, UK
Printed and bound by: Artes Graficas ELKAR S. Coop., Bilbao, Spain

We would like to thank Ethel Davies for the photographs used in this book, to whom the copyright in the photographs belong, with the exception of the following:

Australian Tourist Commission: pages 162 and 167.

Picture research: Deborah Emeny

Acknowledgements: The author would like to thank Avis Rent A Car for assistance given with the research for this guide.